Pinnacle of Desire

By

Joanne Forrest Nutting

Pinnacle of Desire

Copyright ©2009
By Joanne Forrest Nutting

Published by:
Intermedia Publishing Group, Inc.
PO Box 2825
Peoria, AZ 85380
www.intermediapub.com

ISBN 978-1-935529-40-8

PINNACLE OF DESIRE

THE EYE OF GOD

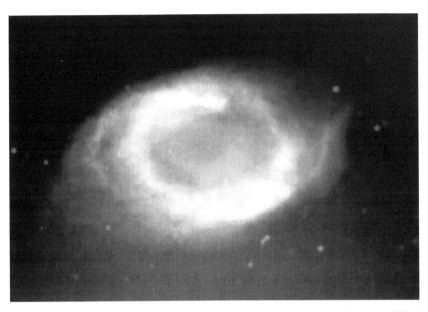

Composite picture is seamless blend of NASA Hubble Space Telescope (HST) images combined view of Mosaic Camera on National Science Foundation's telescope at Kitt Peak National Observatory. Astronomers at Space Telescope Science Institute assembled images into mosaic, and entitled it, "God's Eye."

"I will instruct thee and teach thee in the way which

Thou shalt go: I will guide thee with mine eye."

Psalms 32:8

Contents

Chapter

1. Come Unto Me as Little Children   9

2. Life Is What Happens When You
   Are Doing Something Else   23

3. And When You Are Doing Something
   Else, Life Happens   31

4. Iron Sharpens Iron   43

5. Redeeming the Years the Locusts Had Eaten   53

6. Alone with God   61

7. Teenage to Adult Children   69

8. The Eye of God   79

9. Setting an Example, Opening of the Christian
   Embassy in Washington DC   85

10. Planting a Seed   93

11. God's Faithfulness   101

12. The Comforter Has Come   111

13. The Love of Christ is An Action Illustrated
    through the Love of My Family, Friends,
    and Strangers   125

14. More Pondering God's Angels   133

15. Do the Ones You Love Hurt You the Most?   145

16. A Grandmother's Eyes See Jesus With Singing
    and Rejoicing   157

Study Guide   163

DEDICATION

I dedicate this book to two people who have had great influence in my life.

To my mother, who gave so much of herself to me. (Mama went home to be with Jesus, March, 2008. She was 95 years young! And to my friend Anna Stanley, who was my mentor for some twenty years plus.

Beautiful in every way, Mama taught me so much through her example rather than her words. She illustrated forgiveness and manners and social graces, respect and how to be nice to everyone. Mama was refined and had a great sense of humor. She embarrassed easily, but knew how to take a joke. We were good friends sharing our innermost thoughts and feelings. Mama was not afraid to tell you the truth. She was wise in her advice, only giving it when asked. Mama was a thoughtful and kind grandmother who loved her children and grandchildren, no matter what. Mama loved her sons-in-law and knew how to keep a confidence. She loved the Lord with all of her heart; it was very private and could not talk too much about Jesus without crying. God created Mama beautiful to look at, yet it was her inner beauty that drew people to her. The grace and the glory of the Lord Jesus shone brightly in her eyes and in her example. Mama's life illustrated strength, courage, perseverance. She taught me kindnesses, the error of rudeness, the appreciation of time, and devotion. Mama set an example of service and charity as she gave of her time and money to civic organizations and to our Church. She gave me an appreciation for art, and music, culture and travel. She taught me how to believe and hope and bear hard things. She taught me how to rejoice and dance (Mama knew how to do the Hawaiian Hula), and ice skate; how to ride a horse, and how to dress properly for each occasion. She taught me how to take care of myself; to go to the dentist and doctor, beauty parlor. She loved her garden and her flowers and to dig in the dirt and plant things. She was one of the founding members of Peachtree Battle Garden Club that still exists today. Mama taught me it is my duty to vote and to be a good law abiding citizen. She taught me how to cook and decorate and create a home my family would enjoy and want to come home to everyday. She taught me to love eating mangos, how to fly a kite, to swim and love the ocean. She sat and colored in coloring books with me, played jack stones and pick-up-sticks, Sorry and Monopoly with me. She gave me the love of dogs. She taught me to eat black-eyed peas with chopped onions on top every New Years Day. Mama loved to eat turnip greens and corn bread and vegetables. So do I. Mama loved color and taught me how to "pull things together" with color and space and light. She taught me how to play and have fun; and through example, how to be a mother and a grandmother. Most of all, Mama taught me the truth that has carried me through my journey; the truth that Jesus loves me. Mama always prayed for me when I traveled to serve the Lord. The mother's love given to me was unconditional and I will forever miss her. (Thank you Jesus, for giving me such a chosen one to be my Mother.) So Mama, I hope you are up there in heaven smiling as I honor you and call you blessed.

And to Anna Stanley, who taught me more about how to study the Word of God and how to pray, and be quiet before the Lord, than anyone else God has ever put in my life. Annie, as she is affectionately called, is a gifted teacher and speaker, loved and appreciated by so many. She has been powerfully used of God in my life and in the lives of her students, and especially in the life of her son and daughter, Andy and Becky. (Andy is the Pastor of North Point Community Church, Atlanta, Georgia.) May God bless you extra Annie, for all you have given to me. Not one thing has gone wasted. I honor you in this writing.

Left: Joanne Forrest Nutting

ACKNOWLEDGEMENT

For my treasured life-long friends who have helped me along the way, not just the ones mentioned in this book, but to all the special people God put in my path all through my life. You know who you are! May you finish this journey strong and content. May you enjoy every word of this writing, knowing we are all so deeply blessed by the faithfulness of a righteous God,

and to all the Mothers and Grandmothers of my friends, who helped me; may you receive your reward in heaven for being so good to me, especially Auvern Brady,

to all the Grandmothers in this world who are nurturing and investing their lives in their grandchildren's lives, I pray God will bless you richly as you are used of Him to mold, teach and guide our next generation. And especially to one special Grandmother, Deen Day Sanders, who shares our grandchildren with us; you are God's choice blessing to Madeline, Conner, Darby (and Savannah.) And

5

for the impact your life has had and will continue to have on them, I am deeply and eternally grateful.

For those of you who are not yet believers in Christ as your Savior, or Messiah, I know your God will show you the way he would have you continue on your journey. Keep seeking truth; I am sure you will find the One, who will lead you into all truth, and especially to my husband, John Edward Nutting, J.D., C.C.I.M, and to our children, Bradford James Nutting, Forrest Adelle Nutting Day, Parke Day, Tori Nutting, and our grandchildren, Madeline Day, Conner Day, Darby Day and Savannah Nutting, I give you my heart in this writing. You are right behind Jesus as my finest blessing and reward and have been powerfully used of God to teach me how to see Jesus through a Grandmother's eyes.

PREFACE

Sharing my life's journey, my heart's song with you, has no purpose except to allow you to see that I am not just talking the talk, but have "walked the walk," and in my sharing give you hope that you too will find your heart's song. God has ordered my steps for His purposes of helping others find their way, for His glory. May you be blessed.

Chapter One

COME UNTO ME AS LITTLE CHILDREN

Once upon a time when I was young, I began to ponder the things of God. The things of God, and in life, that seemingly were troubling me, whether small or big; issues in life that my youth could not resolve. God's Word was drawing me, so I began to read. I read more and more, whether in the beauty parlor or a doctor's office or at home in my favorite chair. I could not get enough truth, which somehow I knew held the answers to why my pain was so great.

Somewhere along the way, I had heard someone quote a verse from scripture that went something like this, "Seek me, and you will find me when you seek me with all of your heart." They were quoting the words of Christ, and I had tucked them in the back of my head. These words kept coming back to me, and somehow, I knew it was

God calling me to his side in order to show me the way out of the dark place I was in.

I should tell you, my initial understanding of Christ and my baptism occurred when I was twelve years old while attending Sunday school. However, my real journey began with an awakening of who had gotten hold of me and what had really been made available to me, and in me, in Christ, at age thirty years old. I had attended church and Sunday school all of my life, but at age thirty, a faithful friend, Jackie Beavers, took the time to explain salvation to me. I looked at her through my tears and said, "Why hasn't anyone ever told me this before?" "God lit a fire in my heart that day that burns more brightly each day of my journey with Him. My friend probably saved my life and my marriage through her faithful, pure heart's desire to serve her Jesus. You see, Jackie had only trusted Christ as her Lord and Savior a few months earlier, and admittedly had never been taught how to show someone the way to salvation. She later was pretty funny when we talked about that day. She said, "I was just reading you the tract... God did the rest."

This year, 2009, in October, I will be seventy years young! This gives me some forty years (hard to believe) of putting one foot in front of the other, putting one old memory, one old lie, one old thought at the time, in God's fire and replacing it with the truth of the Word of God which sets us free. Sometimes, my journey has required one step forward, then a step or two backwards. Then I go forward again, facing life knowing Jesus is holding my hand.

At the risk of sounding presumptuous, I would like to try to give you a picture of my life at age 12 when Jesus first called me to his side (Young children have no way of knowing how blessed they are in their circumstances).

Our family lived in a beautiful home on Peachtree Battle Avenue in Atlanta, Georgia. Mama and Daddy had a lady who helped them take care of the house, cooking and my older sister, my younger sister and me. Back then, people called their domestic help a "maid." Her name was Gertrude Griffin, but we affectionately called her "Trudy." We loved Trudy like family. We also had a yardman named Luther, an ironing lady named Iula, a Butler named Charlie, and our beloved cocker spaniel named Bubba. There was always somebody bustling around our house and yard. Daddy owned his own business, his own airplane and he had his own pilot named Butch Seferman. My older sister went to private school and had her own horse that she kept at Judge Gunby's Stables located near Chastain Park. We were given dance lessons, piano lessons, speech lessons and Rich's (Atlanta's premier department store at the time) under the tree every Christmas. We wore beautiful clothes as Mama would take us to Reginstines (a fine clothier) two or three times a year and select five or six new dresses that had the beautiful sashes that tied in the back, for each of we three girls. At Easter, we always got a new dress for Easter Sunday church. Mama and Daddy belonged to two private clubs: The Atlanta Athletic Town Club and the East Lake Country Club. Mama and Daddy took us to Sunday school and church every Sunday whether we wanted to go or not, and afterwards, whether we wanted to go or not, we went out to eat lunch at either Grandma's house or one of the clubs. My sisters and I had no way of knowing everyone did not live as we did. Everyone we knew as little children were just like us. At ages eight and a half and twelve, my younger sister and I did not have opportunity to visit in too many other homes; our neighbors and maybe a classmate or two, but that was it. We were very fortunate and privileged by Atlanta standards, but did not know it. Mama and Daddy were always entertaining, which kept Trudy and Charlie busy cooking and cleaning silver, or getting formally dressed to attend some social affair in Atlanta. We were normal, happy kids, or so it seemed.

It all began that horrible day when my Mother and Father called us into the den, sat us down and explained to us they were going to get a divorce. Remember, I was just 12 years old, Joy was 17 years old, and Susan was 81/2. We were not sure what all this meant, but we did know it meant that Daddy would be leaving home. This was all I needed to know to scar me for the rest of my life.

Mama seemed very irritable; not herself. She seemed to be on her last nerve, having little patience with us. Our house was a two story, white painted brick house with Buckhead green (black/green) shutters. At the top of the steps upstairs, there was a large landing. Mama had a placed a sofa on the landing where you could sit and look out the window. We liked to sit there and watch the cars go by on Northside Drive, which at that time was the main artery to town. (There was no I-75 or I-85 built yet.) I used to get behind the sofa and play with my dolls and sometimes use it as a hiding place if I didn't want to be found when Mama or Trudy called me to come to them.

One Sunday morning when I did not want to go to church I heard Mama call me to come in her room. It was time to get my hair brushed with ribbon tied in. I hid behind the sofa and did not respond to her call. She came looking for me. When she saw my arm sticking out she said, "Sister, (my family calls me, "Sister") come out of there, you are going to make us late!" I still did not respond, so Mama grabbed my arm, pulled me and I resisted. She was already on her last nerve and this pushed her over the edge. She pulled again, this time I was out from behind the sofa and Mama hit me over the head with the hairbrush so hard the brush broke in half. Did I deserve to be punished? Yes. Should she have hit me over the head? No.

My head hurt, but my Spirit was wounded. A stripe was put on my little mind that day, and remained until I was well in my forties. I felt a sense of betrayal by the one who was supposed to have loved me and protected me, no matter what. Mama was no longer my "safe place." Daddy was gone. A seed of bitterness took root in my heart that day. A wall between Mama and me existed from then on. Everything that went wrong in my life was attached to Mama somehow.

Hair brushed and bow tied in, off we went to Sunday school where I learned that Jesus Loves Me.

Daddy and I were so very close. He was so proud of me; he insisted I be named after him even though I was not the son he had hoped for. Daddy and I did everything together. He took me to his office and on business trips with him. I sat in his lap at night while listening to the radio and sat next to him to watch television. When our family went somewhere in the car, I was sitting right next to Daddy (In those days there were no seat belts and a child could sit in the middle of the front seat). You get the picture.

The day Daddy had to leave, I found myself standing in the front yard crying as I watched him put his few belongings in the car. (I thought it strange that the car held all that Daddy owned in the whole world. This didn't seem right.) Nevertheless, my heart broke

14

as I watched my Father, my friend, my protector, my pal, drive out the driveway.

Soon, the next horrible thing happened. We were told our forever-faithful friend and servant Trudy was going to go to work for Daddy and would be leaving us. Trudy had been by my side everyday of my life. Seriously, Trudy was there the day I was brought home from the hospital, slept in our basement all those twelve years and was with us 24/7. For us to lose Trudy after losing Daddy felt like our world was being pulled apart. I loved Trudy with all my heart; she was part of our family. I didn't know what I would do without her hugs and kisses, her great food, her laughter and love towards us. Trudy did everything for us... what would we do without her? Soon I realized Iula was not there, nor Charlie or Luther. Everybody was gone.

Insecurity began to set in as reality hit us all in the face. Daddy did not come through the door at night with a smile, candy or a stick of gum, and a big hug. Mama decided we had to sell the house and move into a smaller one, so now my back yard tree house and badminton court were going to be gone. All this sounds trivial to me now as I write about it, but to a twelve year old who had never experienced any other way of life, it was devastating. Even my neighborhood friends, who I rode bikes with nearly every day, would be too far away from our new house to see very often. Things would never be the same.

The next year in school, there were many changes, all significant. Everyone changed schools, starting High School in the 8th Grade. I was 13. Entering a new school, becoming a teenager, having to wash my own clothes, moving into a smaller house, not having any money to go to the movies, not having Trudy there to talk to, having to ride the bus to school instead of Mama taking us, and no shopping trips for new clothes for the first time – it all seemed too much at once. Somehow, in my young mind, I thought all this was my mother's fault. I could not understand why she and Daddy could not have just worked things out for us. At age 13, it is "all about you." (Can you see how children's lives are formed and damaged through life experiences?)

Mama, my sisters and I began to argue about everything. What I did not know, but soon found out was that Mama was very sick. She had pernicious anemia and was dying. Her doctor told her she did not have enough red blood cells left in her body to be alive and he could not understand why she was still living. The stress of daddy's verbal, emotional, mental and physical abuse had beaten Mama down to a mere shell of a person. Daddy was a wonderful, loving, generous, thoughtful, successful man until he took his first drink of alcohol. Daddy served in World War I when he was sixteen or seventeen years old, which left him emotionally damaged. He was fearful and slept with a loaded pistol under the mattress every night. Alcohol seemed to unleash his pent up emotions and turned him into a person we did not know. Daddy became abusive in every way when intoxicated. Daddy did not ever want me to see or know this part of him. Only once did he hurt me. I have never forgotten the switching I received.

Daddy had lied to all of their friends to cover his own behavior. He embarrassed Mama publically and soon all of Buckhead society knew our family was having problems. (Buckhead is a prominent area of Atlanta, Georgia. The Governor's Mansion is located there as well as some of Atlanta's most beautiful homes. Many of Atlanta's most prominent people lived in Buckhead back in those days.") Mama had been active in so many civic organizations, Rabun Gap, Dogwood Festival, etc. and was a founding member of Peachtree Battle Garden Club. She was known and well thought of among her peers. But now, Mama began to withdraw, and after eighteen years of the stress Daddy had put on her, Mama filed for a divorce. Her health was so severely damaged she had to send us away for the summer so she could get some rest and try to get well. The stress of divorce, moving, giving up everything in her life she had known for eighteen years, had taken a very severe toll on her. Mama had to do what she had to do. I did not get it then, but of course, I get it now!

My Aunt, Mama's sister, came to visit us with her daughter, our first cousin. We loved our Aunt, Uncle and cousin and spent time with them as often as we could as they lived in Birmingham, Alabama. Every summer though, Mama made a point of us spending time together, so it was great that they had come for a visit!

What we didn't know was that Mama had made an arrangement to send Susan and me to Birmingham with Aunt "G" for the whole summer. Our older sister stayed with Mama. Things kept getting sprung on us without warning that were such a shock all we could do was cry. I still remember, and can draw a visual in my mind, the day Aunt "G's" car pulled away from the curb with my sister and me in the back seat. I had the window rolled down, was hanging out of the window looking at Mama standing on the front step waving to us, as I was yelling to her through my tears, "Mama, P L E A S E don't make us go." All Mama could do was stand there and cry. We still had not been told how sick Mama was. Guess they thought we were too young and it would just worry us and make things worse.

Summer ended and Mama came to Birmingham to get us. God had protected her. His mercies were fresh every morning. She was strong enough to come and get us. We had as good a time with our cousin and Aunt as one could possibly have had with the amount of sadness we were carrying in our hearts. Our Aunt tried her best to care for and love us. I am sure it was not easy taking on two more little children for so long a time. Luckily, our cousin, being an only child, had a million toys and games and tri-cycles to play with. Her maid was there and Grandma was there, as well as our Uncle, so it wasn't as though we were suffering. Nevertheless, we were so happy to get home and back to our own rooms and stuff, and Mama. If only I had known my Heavenly Father had not left me and was right there with me.

My first day in the eighth grade at Northside High School, (the public high school for our area) was fun. I got to see all my seventh grade friends, meet some new friends, meet the Coach in the gym and learn there was Cheerleading offered. They also had Clubs you could join and it seemed everyone had grown up somehow, all the boys looked different. This is when I first met a new boy named Ed. He was a tall person, sweet face, and very friendly. He was too cocky for me, but nice enough. Anyway, I already sort of had a crush on another boy.

Ed wasted no time getting to know me and asked if I was going on the hayride our class was having. I said yes, and he smiled and said he was too. This began a very long courting relationship that God must have had his hand on. How can any two thirteen year olds have a friendship and an attraction that would last a lifetime? Ed and I married at age 21 and have been married for forty-seven years. He is the only man I have ever wanted and ever truly loved. Yes, I had a few crushes, dates and kisses along the way, but my heart belonged to Ed and still does.

(As a footnote, I would like to add, any woman who was or is serving God by serving her fellow man as a servant, "a maid," my heart wonders if you truly understand what a high calling God has put on your life. The love and companionship your life gives to the family you are serving will only be fully known when you get to heaven. I salute you and say "thank you" to you, for all you have and are giving to enrich the life of another. My Trudy's position in my life gave her the right to invest her life into my life as no person outside our family could ever have had. Often times the female servant in the home is a better friend to the "lady of the house" than the friends in her social circle. A servant sees and hears all that goes on inside the home. They see your life and your children's lives at the best, and at the worst. They know the "real you," and are faithful to try and help you, no matter what. They see the abuse and their hearts understand and try to comfort you. Unfortunately, the servant is experiencing the emotion of pain right along side you, and most of all, a true servant knows how to keep the confidences or secrets of the family. They never tell anyone, anyone, about your personal life.)

(Trudy's investment in me as a child gave me the strength through her love, to face the trials of my life. She knew when my heart ached and gave me those hugs I so desperately needed. I know my Trudy has a special place in heaven, right beside God, as all will who have been given the high calling of a Servant.)

Gertrude Griffin

Chapter Two

LIFE IS WHAT HAPPENS WHEN YOU ARE DOING SOMETHING ELSE

The years to come were filled with good and bad. My life was like a yoyo, going back and forth, up and down. In the tenth grade Mama moved us to Florida. My heart broke a second time as I had to leave Ed, my friends, cheerleading, gymnastics and my neighborhood. God's faithfulness continued as I adjusted in a new environment, school, and made new friends, joined a sorority and modern dance club. The people there were very nice to me and I did enjoy my friendships and experiences.

Yet my heart was still with Ed.

By now, some two years later, Mama decided she needed to move us closer to her sister. Mama was having a hard time financially and needed family, so she moved us to Birmingham, Alabama. We lived with my Aunt and cousin until Mama could obtain a job and get back on her feet. Again, I had to uproot, leave my friends and start over. Shades Valley High School was the public school for our area. We were in a nice neighborhood in Birmingham, which was my last stop before I graduated from high school. Mama did, however, allow me to fly back to Florida and graduate with my classmates there; although I took my last classes in Birmingham, I am a graduate of Coral Gables Senior High School.

I knew there would be no money for me to go to college like my friends were doing, no sorority, no Junior League, so at age 17 I took a job in Atlanta and left home to go out on my own. Mama cried when I left, telling me she was not quite ready for me to leave home, but I thought I was ready. I wanted to be closer to Ed.

I stayed with Daddy until I could find a place I could afford. There was no money for a car so I took a room in a lady's apartment who worked at the same place I did. She was kind enough to give me a ride to and from work everyday. Her name was Mrs. Carter, a very nice woman. Ed was attending Georgia Tech on a football scholarship. The syrup plant for The Coca Cola Company, where I worked, was down the street from Georgia Tech on North Avenue, so we got to see each other now and then during the day, and on weekends, Ed was able to use his family car and take me out on dates. We managed until I saved my money and was able to buy a used car. We were so happy. All we had, literally, was each other, and that seemed to be all we needed. God was working in my life to mould and shape my circumstances, so that I would realize my need for a closer walk with Him. My journey continued though I was still ignorant of Christ's Spirit presence and faithfulness in my life.

I did not really know who Mr. Robert Woodruff was. I just knew he was the "Big Top Boss" at Coca Cola. I would see him occasionally as he would come into our department to see an executive. Each time he would pass by my desk, I would always make a point of looking up and saying "hello, Mr. Woodruff." After all, Mama had taught me manners and respect, and Daddy had taken me to his office so many times, I kind of knew how it went when company arrived. So being my friendly self, I just spoke up when Mr. Woodruff walked by. Everyone else kept their heads down hard at work, but that just wasn't me. He must have noticed my good manners and when an opening came for the Receptionist on his Executive Floor, he asked my boss if I typed well, and of course, I did. I taught myself when I was young at Daddy's office and had been practicing for several years just because I enjoyed it. I was promoted to be the Receptionist of Mr. Woodruff's Executive Suite when I was eighteen years old.

Mr. Woodruff and his staff were very polite to me explaining my job duties and showing me around, introducing me to each Executive there so when a guest arrived, I would know where to show them in. They also included me in social gatherings in their homes, as well as lunches in the private dining room. Howard, the cook, realized I was a child, as did all the other older people I was working for, and he too was very nice to ask me if I liked the food before putting it on my plate.

Because it is kind of interesting, I will inject two memories I have while working for Mr. Woodruff. The day I was asked to type Mr. Woodruff's Federal Income Tax return. Even back then, those numbers seemed so big they went right over my head. I didn't have a clue what I was typing and to this day could not tell you what was on the Return. All I remember is those were some long, big numbers.

The second memory was the day of a Coca Cola Board of Directors Meeting. The Board Room was located in a huge room right down the hall from my desk. A guest arrived wearing a big white turban on his head. I had never seen anyone dressed like this except in the movies, but I was polite and showed the gentleman into the Boardroom. Another guest arrived, a husky, tall, distinguished looking man. As I was showing him into the Boardroom he asked me for an aspirin. I said, "Yes Sir, I will be right back with one." Upon my return with the aspirin, I walked over to the sideboard, poured a drink of water and took the water and the aspirin to the gentleman. He said, "Thank you" and I went back to my desk.

Later, I learned two things; one, this man was James Farley, Post Master General of the United States of America (a close friend of President Roosevelt;) and secondly, women were never allowed in the Board Room…which I had not been told, (Oh My…. how things have changed since then.) Once again, I knew Jesus was ordering my steps and showing me things of which I knew not.

A year went by and I was happy. Then the phone rang one Saturday morning while I was at home in Mrs. Carter's apartment. It was my stepmother. She was crying and told me Daddy had been killed in an automobile accident the night before while on his way home from a business trip. A truck had entered his lane of traffic while going around a parked vehicle on the side of the road and sheared off the front of the car on the driver's side. My little brother, Robert, who was only five years old, was in the car with Daddy and witnessed my father's body being broken and bleeding. Robert was not physically hurt, but emotionally his little life had a stripe put on it, like the stripes Jesus bore at his crucifixion. It was dark when the accident occurred and Robert was taken home with some woman who lived near the accident site until my stepmother could get to South Georgia to retrieve him. Of course, this little boy was terrified. They took Daddy to the nearest hospital, where later that evening, he went home to be with Jesus.

All of this happened so fast, there was no time for a phone call for me to go to South Georgia with my stepmother. I never saw my father alive again.

I truly believe God saw Daddy's life all the way throughout eternity and knew it best to remove him from this earth. As sad and heart broken as I was, and as hard as it was for me to overcome my feelings of loss, I know now that Daddy's alcoholic behavior would have spilled out onto my stepbrother and my half brother. It had already harmed my stepbrother once, and I believe when this happened, God said, "This is enough."

I don't think God planned Daddy's accident. He would not do that to my little brother Robert. But I do believe God allows man's mistakes to end in disaster sometimes. When a ten ton truck shaves off the whole driver's side of your heavy Fleetwood Cadillac, you have great opportunity to become a statistic. It must have been Daddy's time to go. I don't know. I was nineteen years old, and devastated.

I knew enough about the love of Christ and his forgiveness to know my Daddy was in heaven. I knew Daddy loved the Lord no matter how damaged his emotions were from War. I also knew Christ's death on the Cross had forgiven him all his sins.

My Daddy

Chapter Three

AND WHILE YOU ARE DOING SOMETHING ELSE LIFE HAPPENS

At age 21 Ed and I married. Again, happy times were upon us. We were truly in love, and because Ed had been drafted as the Cleveland Browns Football Team's second draft choice, he now had a way to financially support a wife. I was able to give up my job, and off I went to Cleveland, Ohio, to begin my life with the man I loved.

As I fast forward to age thirty, Ed and I have two children by now; a son named Brad, age 2 ½, and our newborn little girl named Adelle. We had bought our first home and Ed had finished his career in Pro-football. After having played for the Cleveland Browns for one year and the Dallas Cowboys for two years, Ed had torn the cartilage in his knee and decided he would rather be able to walk the rest of his life than to play football any longer. Now we were facing the realization of having to earn a living as all of our friends were. We had savings, so Ed decided he would start a career in commercial real estate. Both of our fathers were deceased so we had no one to give us any guidance. We had suffered through the loss of our second son during the fifth month of pregnancy before our daughter was born, and I was very sick with ulcerated colitis. Ed was full of life, strong, happy and neither of us realized how frayed my nerves were. There was a lot of yelling going on in our house, and a lot of love.

This brings us back to the day my friend Jackie explained salvation to me and began to disciple me. My world was falling apart. I needed help. The twenty-two pills a day that the doctors had me taking were only making me feel worse. Azulfidine is a Sulphur drug that saps all of your energy. I could hardly get the children taken care of and get dinner on the table. Things were not good. Jackie would call me and say "I'll pick you up tomorrow at 10am. And wear a dress." I didn't even ask her where we were going. I trusted her to be taking me to learn something that would help me. This went on several times a week for three years! Can you believe Jackie's faithfulness? Jackie had a friend named Grace Kinser. Grace held a bible study in her home every week with a teacher from Chattanooga, Tennessee, teaching different books of the bible. The teacher's name was Kay Arthur. Every week for several years, Kay drove from Chattanooga to Atlanta, Georgia, to teach us. A faithful servant of God. To this day, I am grateful for Kay's teaching and discipleship.

A year or so later I even started a bible study at my house and guess who agreed to teach it? Yes, Jackie. As I struggled to put one foot in front of the other during those days, my faith began to build. I had learned at Church to read Proverbs and Psalms everyday, so I did. I laugh now because here I was in a ditch, and a couple of the first Proverbs I ever read were Proverbs 21:9, "It is better to dwell in a corner of the housetop, than with a brawling woman in a wide house," and 21:19, "It is better to dwell in the wilderness, than with a contentious and an angry woman."

I thought, "Oh great, this is encouraging!" My heart knew I was that brawling and contentious woman. My bad attitude was the first very clear illustration of my life not lining up with God's word. This was obviously God's voice speaking specifically to me. I had some changing to do, but of course did not know how. I kept putting one foot in front of the other. Kept reading God's word, kept going to bible study and Church.

Then another issue would come up, like the children and Ed being so messy and taking so much of my energy to keep up with my perfectionism. I was fussy and out of sorts with them. When they spilled their little cup of milk on the floor, I yelled at them. Poor kids, they were so little and I was expecting way too much. Ed didn't listen to me anyway so my fussing was like water off a duck's back. He would just say something funny, hug me and go on his way, but there was no help, and no change.

 Again, I cried out to the Lord to help me. He took me to another verse in Proverbs, 14:4; "Where no oxen are, the crib is clean: but much increase is by the strength of the ox." I heard God's voice loud and clear saying, "If something happened to take your husband and children away from here, it would take you about 30 minutes to clean up after them. Their rooms would be clean and empty forevermore."

The scripture set me straight. Again, it was my problem. I argued with God saying, "But Lord, I was seeking you for change in my husband and children. And now you are telling me again, I am the one with the bad attitude that needs changing." I had to agree with God. He was right. The thing that bugged me a little was he is always right! I just had to start agreeing with him. My hard head and stubborn ways were not getting me what I really wanted, which was to feel good again and be a happy Mom and wife.

 How can a baby and a two-year-old keep their rooms clean all the time? Moreover, isn't a wife supposed to be her husband's helpmate? (Can you hear the frustration of a young mother's cry for resolve?) I told myself I "should be" making up the bed and cleaning the kitchen, etc. As Mama used to say, "What is wrong with you?" (This is what I call taking one of those steps backwards on my journey.) Yet, I had an attitude change the minute I agreed with God and changed my mind to line up with his thinking.

I was beginning to see how this thing called life worked. Every painful issue in my life that was unresolved had a solution in God's word. I had brought a lot of baggage into our marriage from my childhood. All that pain I shared with you earlier came right in the door with us on our wedding night. Poor Ed had also brought a lot of baggage through the door with him, but we will talk about that in another chapter.

In our Church on Sunday mornings at the end of the service, the Pastor gives an Altar call. That is, he asks if there is anyone in the service who would like to come forward to the Altar and give their hearts and lives to Christ. Not all churches do this, but ours did, every Sunday. By now, I needed someone to explain some things to me in the Bible I did not really understand when reading alone. So I marched myself right up front at the Altar call and told the Pastor I needed help understanding the Bible and wanted to know how he did that. I am sure his heart was chuckling at my ignorance, and at my bravery. I felt like a bad child when he told me to go to the office in the Church and wait there until the service was ended. He would be glad to get me some help. So I did, and sure enough, they gave me a list of concordances, and helpful books to aid me in my quest to better know God. I had the nerve to ask the Pastor which Bible he used. I knew it was a King James, but which one? He was very patient with me as I wrote down the name of his Bible.

Please understand, growing up, Daddy was an Elder in our church and our Pastor and his wife ate dinner in our home pretty often. Mama and Daddy had traveled to Mexico by car with them, shared old movies of the trip in our downstairs playroom, and otherwise fellowshipped together, so I was not afraid of a Pastor. He was a friend in my mind, and this Pastor and his wife became Ed's and my good friends over the years. In fact, his wife became a very close friend. They saw two people hungry to know God and took us under their wing.

I will forever be grateful for the hours and years we spent together talking about Christ and how to better study and understand the Word of God. They prayed with us and through their example showed us how to pray as we searched God's word and wisdom for our lives. We had fun traveling together, going sailing up on Lake Lanier together, genuinely enjoying the journey of faith and fun. Their investment in our lives for eternity, has been and is being used of God however He directs.

So we were off to the Christian Book Store to get some help and it was great. I am still using the New Thompson Chain Reference

Bible Fourth Improved Edition King James Version, recommended to me that day. I have used about every kind of Bible printed over these forty years, but I still love my Thompson Chain. (This past Christmas I purchased one for our daughter and found out they are not printing this Bible any longer. By the grace of God, I obtained a copy of their Special Anniversary Edition of which they had only a few copies.)

I was excited and ready to get started with all my new books. After getting the children off to school, deciding what was for dinner and getting that organized, making up the beds, etc., I would dig in reading. Guess what? I found that scripture I told you about that had gotten stuck in my head way back there years before. The one that says, "But if from thence thou shalt seek the Lord thy God, thou shalt find him, if thou seek him with all thy heart and with all thy soul." It was in Deuteronomy 4:29. I was thrilled to find something familiar and positive that encouraged me.

I kept reading and later came to a verse in Hosea 10:12. You ask why I am jumping around in my reading, rather than just reading the Bible through. Well, this great Bible that I had just purchased had all these reference verses in the margin that pertain to what you are reading and when I read them it helped me understand what I was trying to read in the first place. It took me hours to do this, but my fire was burning brightly.

Hosea 10:12 says, "Sow to yourselves in righteousness, reap in mercy: break up your fallow ground: for it is time to seek the Lord, till he come and rain righteousness upon you." Wow, this spoke to my heart. I knew I needed to break up my fallow ground, and I knew if I kept trying, God would help me do so.

Because every reference I encountered kept implying it my duty to seek after God, I knew my eyes and my mind would be opened to the truth and would show me how my personal life could heal and be made whole again. My heart knew God longed to give me the desires of my heart, yet I must not procrastinate when he showed me truth that would help me become free. I must put action to my thoughts and feelings; I must take time to find the buried feelings that were owned by the thought that was causing me pain. I knew this wasn't going to be quick, and I knew it was not going to be easy.

It was during these years of searching with all my heart, earnestly seeking the heart of God, spending hours studying God's Word, that our Church announced the Billy Graham Crusade was coming to Atlanta. I think this was the summer of 1972. Our children wanted to go to the Crusade and Ed and I thought it important to take them.

We drove downtown, parked in a Hotel parking lot near the stadium where the crusade was to be held and went inside to have dinner in the restaurant before attending the Crusade. As we walked down a hallway to the restaurant we passed by some elevators. Just at that moment the elevator opened and out walked Billy Graham and Cliff Barrows. We were so shocked, all we could do was to say, "Hello," and keep walking.

The waitress seated us, we ordered dinner, ate and were ready to leave when we noticed a lady sitting at the next table who had her hair up in a bun in the back. I asked Ed if that was Corrie Ten Boon. He looked and said, "I believe it is." She turned her head just enough for me to confirm this was Corrie Ten Boom. She too was finished with her meal so as we departed, we stopped at her table and we introduced ourselves to her and told her how very much we had appreciated her book The Hiding Place. She looked me straight in the eye and said to me, "Prepare to suffer my dear, before you die." Her words were so moving and so much bigger than I was, I could only tuck them in the back of my mind for safekeeping, forever. We said our goodbye's and headed out the door for the Crusade.

The stadium was completely full. Our children sat on the edge of their seats listening to every word Dr. Graham had to say. Brad was nine and one-half and Adelle was seven years old. I had not expected them to be so interested, and yet Brad had been unusually interested in hearing the Word of God at Church. When the invitation came to come forward, as is always given at the Billy Graham Crusades, Brad insisted we go forward. I gave the excuse there were so many people that maybe we shouldn't try to go so far in such a crowd. He would not take no for an answer! I heard Brad say, "Mom, we have to go... now." So I took a deep breath and down we went. Brad and Adelle prayed to receive Christ that night. My heart was again overflowing with gratitude for the faithfulness of my Jesus. "The children were so young," I thought. But I celebrated with them all the way home!

A week or so later, Ed and I decided to invite our Pastor and his wife over for lunch so they could question and talk to the children to be sure they understood their salvation. At the end of their visit, they agreed both children clearly understood that they had given their hearts to Jesus as their Savior and they were ready to be baptized.

Oh how God was working in our family. I was more motivated than ever to study God's Word so I could answer my children's questions as they began to grow in Christ, so I went back to the bookstore! My life seemed to be taking one step back and two steps forward. All I knew in my heart, was, I had to keep trying and learning. My children's names were written in the Lamb's Book of Life! Again, I was singing and praising and rejoicing, in all humility.

Forrest and Ed on their wedding day

Ed and Brad (Pals)

Adelle and Mom (Forrest)
"Dad's two girls."

Chapter Four

IRON SHARPENS IRON

The further I continued on my journey to seek our Lord, the harder things got. The ulcerated colitis lead pipe condition in my body had miraculously been healed as I allowed God's truth to bring peace to my stressful life. Yes, it had taken five years to undo the physical damage my emotions had done to my physical being. The faithfulness of God was growing so strong in my heart it was undeniable.

By now, the children are old enough to be of help and are a complete delight, Ed is soaring with the eagles in the prime of his career in commercial real estate, and decides he would like to go back to school and get a law degree. He thought this would help him in real estate and he loved to read and learn. Of course I agreed to night school after work, but didn't have a clue what I was about to get myself into. I am putting on a good face, but there still seems to be a semi-war going on inside of me. I am restless because I still have unforgiveness in my heart. I felt like David when he wrote in the Psalms "How long wilt thou forget me, O Lord? Forever? How long wilt thou hide thy face from me? How long shall I take counsel in my soul, having sorrow in my heart daily?" (Psalm 13:1-2, The New Thompson Chain-Reference Bible, Fourth Improved Edition, King James Version)

During the long days and nights without my husband, I began more Bible study classes on different subjects I was interested in. I volunteered at Church to help with the ladies socials, read books, and whatever I could do to fill the time. I helped the children as much as I could with their homework, and had spend the night parties over and over again, mostly for Adelle and her friends, which was so much fun. I helped lead a Cub Scout Troop for Brad and his friends, which was a great time. The boys seemed to enjoy their new adventures. I joined a prayer group at Church where I experienced how to pray out loud, gaining a sense of being comfortable just talking to Jesus as I prayed for other people's needs. Christ was becoming my friend as well as my Lord and Savior.

Ed was gone five nights a week and needed supper at 10 P.M. when he got home. I was overseeing all the children's homework, cooking dinner and eating with the kids, going to their sports activities, etc. without Ed. Our children are not getting to see their father and are begging to stay up late until he gets home. They are feeling abandoned. Stress, and more stress keeps me on my knees in prayer. I am lonely, doing our laundry at night to pass the time. Our schedule is totally disrupted. Ed is doing his homework from 10:30 at night until midnight, then getting up and going to work the next morning. He is certainly to be commended for the huge effort he put into not only finishing law school, but also passing the Georgia Bar Exam on the first try. Congratulations Ed! We are all very proud of you.

We had weathered the storm of Ed's absence, but the children were acting out their pain, and Ed was so controlling of my every move. He must have sensed he was losing control during his long months of preoccupation with work, school and studies.

Once again, I hear God's small voice saying to me, "Get hold of your self, dear one. This is your problem. Life is not all about you." I think to myself, "Okay, Lord. Who am I mad with? Why can't I forgive my Mother for divorcing my Daddy? Why can't I forgive those who have hurt me?" "That memory of Mama hitting me so hard over the head with the hairbrush keeps coming back every time she does something to aggravate me. And Ed's stubborn tight fist with our money aggravates me. I think I will just go out and get a job! After all Brad is twelve years old now and Adelle 9-1/2. They are practically grown." (God hears our cries of desperation, sadness from deferred hope, and loneliness, when no one else is listening.)

So, off I go for an interview with Eastern Air Lines to become a flight attendant. What happened to that good path I was on? I kept thinking maybe this would give direction to my life and I would be happier. Maybe I will find my answers if I can just get away from all this for a while. I knew I did not want a divorce, but I also knew something had to give. I was not happy and God had already told me this was "my problem." I am sure God was looking down on me saying, "This one is going to suffer some more before she wills to see me more clearly."

I left home for Eastern Air Lines flight attendant training school, which was held in Miami, Florida. My sister was a teacher at the training school and was very instrumental in getting me hired. The Women's Equal Rights Amendment was in the forefront during this time and Eastern was required to hire a few "married, older women." I was now thirty-eight years old, and married. I fit the criteria they were looking for and my body weight and height were acceptable. I have my sister to thank for all she did to help me back then. She and my brother-in-law have always been my cheerleaders. They have loved me, no matter what. Thank you Jesus for the incredible, loving, forgiving family you have given me as a gift. What would I do without them?

Our children managed somehow, but were beginning to show more signs of insecurity and sadness. Ed was so shocked over my choice to take this job; he had to go for counseling. In his mind, I had left him and the children and he didn't know how to handle it. Was God at work in my life? Of course he was. Was I just trying to survive? Of course I was. It is so clear to me now how sins are passed down from generation to generation. We repeat what we know, bad or good, the sins of learned behavior. Only now, not only Ed had left the children, but their Mom was also leaving for two whole months – as I had seen my Father leave me. I searched God's Word daily for more resolve. Though I could not see it with my eyes, He was at work in my heart through the hearts of our children.

About a year into being hard at work flying all over the United States, it was becoming apparent my being gone was not the best thing for our family. Even my dentist made a comment I have remembered all these years, "If Ed were taking really good care of you, you would not be gone." Wow, this shocked me that an outsider could see through what was going on. I spent every waking moment I could with the children, but they had to go to school and Ed and I had to go to work. The children needed more, so I knew then my job would come to an end. It was just a matter of time.

Some insights I gleaned during this experience are very valuable to me. I saw people who were hurting out there in the world. So many young beautiful girls sleeping around – some having abortions – and drinking too much; young employees stealing liquor off of the service carts on the airplane; people who had absolutely lost their way. I began talking to them about Jesus. There were long trips that lasted four hours sometimes and we could sit on the jump seat and talk (the jump seat is where the flight attendants sit for take off and landings). I began to have opportunities to lead others to Christ and help them find resolution to problems that Jesus had given to me for my life. In fact, the day I gave my resignation to my Supervisor at Eastern, she said to me, "You are so brave, I wish I had the nerve to quit this job and go home."

I realized God had again done a work in my life, even in my rebellion. Counseling others had now become comfortable for me so I decided to go for some formal training. Grace Fellowship International was holding a seminar at our Church. A man named Dr. Solomon was coming to speak, so I decided to attend. They offered a one-day course, a three-day course and a two-month Internship. I attended them all. Graduation was most gratifying. As other people's needs motivated me to sharpen my God given skills, again I saw Jesus at work in my life, my husband's life, our children's lives as well as my whole family. Tom Grady and Duane

Farmer, my instructors, were powerfully used of God in my life. Thank you, Lord.

By now, my Mother and my younger sister had moved back to Atlanta and were living close by. My friend phoned me one day and informed me there was going to be a lady speaking at her Church who had a reputation of being really funny and she was using her humor to lead people to Christ. Jackie asked if I would like to go. I said yes and asked if I may bring my mother and my sister. "Of course," she replied.

Mama and my sister accepted my invitation, so off to hear this lady we went. I could not tell you one thing she said except something about a cabbage and peeling off the leaves of the cabbage having something to do with people finding their way, and that she was very funny, yet serious. But when the program was over and we were walking out of the building on the way through the parking lot to the car, I heard my sister say, "Well, I gave my heart to Jesus tonight."

Mama chimed right in and said, "I gave my heart to Him too, and I know I am forgiven." With great gusto she added, "I feel saved!" She was walking like she was ten pounds lighter and the remainder of the way to the car and all the way home, my sister and my mother could not stop praising their new found love and appreciation for

Christ. Needless to say, again my God had shown Himself faithful and my heart was singing and rejoicing in what He had done through the humor of this lady. My mother and my sister had their names written in the Lamb's Book of Life, forevermore. I continued to have my faith strengthened that night, as I again stood in awe of Holy God and His goodness.

Even when we are in the middle of storms in our own lives, if we will just keep putting one foot in front of the other and remain faithful to seek after the heart of God and take a few people along with us, He will do the rest!

"Forrest's Graduating Class Eastern Air Lines Flight Attendant School

51

Chapter Five

REDEEMING THE YEARS THE LOCUSTS HAD EATEN

The love of our children took root in my heart the first minute I looked at them the day they were born. I have never looked back. They have been and are the most important people in Ed's and my lives. We love them so much we would give our lives for them without hesitation. In fact, in a way, this is what we have always done, give our lives for our children… or so we thought. The first thing I wanted to do when I gave up my job with Eastern Airlines, was to go home and pick up the pieces from my having been gone.

We car pooled the children to school, were there to pick them up, take them to sports, have friends come over to play and spend the night. Whatever they wanted to do or needed to do pretty much would dictate our lives. The parents of their friends became our circle of friends. Ed and I enjoyed our children as much as any parents could. I believe somewhere during this time a seed of guilt took root. We were subconsciously feeling guilty for having been absent in their lives. We thought we owed the children something and began to over indulge them. (This was some kind of payback.) Any time we scolded or spanked them, we felt horrible and would later do something to try and make up for it even though they deserved to be punished. The children were getting mixed signals from us and, I am sure, were learning how to manipulate us. I question whether we were teaching them the world owed them something, or that life was "all about them."

I wish I had known as a young mother what I know now as a grandmother. We made so many mistakes through the years that, only by the grace of God, have been redeemed. Our adult children love us unconditionally, so I guess we did one thing right, we loved them. God's Word says, "Love Never Fails."

Our journey included some hard knock lessons I would like to pass along to young mothers. I would have given anything if someone had told me these things when our children were young. My mother probably tried to help me, but my rebellious spirit towards her caused me to reject her words when she tried.

First suggestion, Listen to your children. Their words are important to them and are a part of their self respect.

Remember, you are the parent. They are the child. Bend down to their level, look them in the eye and talk to them when they are upset. Don't let them set the boundaries, for their sake. Guide them with your leadership.

Put your children in "Time Out" when they need discipline. Try never to provoke them to anger, and especially try never to hit them, especially if you are angry. This never gives you the results you are hoping for.

Give yourself a time out if you feel out of control. Follow through after you regain your composure.

Forgive quickly. Teach them forgiveness is for them, not for the other person. We forgive in obedience to Christ, which sets us free from guilt. Christ issues the punishment to the offender.

Stick up for your child when he or she is having a conflict with another adult. If the conflict does not happen in your presence, go back to the offending adult with them as soon as possible. Make it right. This builds your child's self esteem, as they have no guilt over the incident. It doesn't matter whether in school or at a friends house, where ever. Adults outside the family have no right to embarrass your child or yell at them. They certainly have no right to pinch, shove or hit them. We have laws against this now, but when our children were young, on occasion their teacher would yell at our children in front of the class and humiliate them rather than pull them aside and talk to them one on one. This is unacceptable. Your child's dignity and respect are at risk. Ed and I had to go to the children's school several times to confront a teacher, sometimes with the principal present. There was always an apology made to the child, not just to us. Once a teacher threw a desk across the room he was so out of control. Another time, the teacher was passing condoms around the room for the children to hold and see. If our children had not come home and told us what happened we could not have corrected the situation.

Keep an open line of communication no matter what it takes. I recall the day I had to choose between being "right" and "having a relationship with our daughter." The day she turned 13, it seemed every day was an argument to get her way about something. I weighed each argument, and allowed her to decide as often as I possibly could. Most of it was not important anyway, but seemed to help her grow in her decision making.

Try never to separate your children in the schools they attend. I am not talking about Lower School vs. Middle School and Upper School. I am talking about sending one to a completely different school on a different campus. This was one of our most regretful mistakes. One child was doing well in private school. The other was not doing so well and was having a hard time that year with friends. The Head Master called us in like we were bad children and suggested if we wanted this struggling child to remain in his school, perhaps we should consider giving a donation to the school. Ed and I were insulted by his bullying and did not quite know what to do. Rather than seeking solutions to these temporary problems with counselors, tutors, etc., we took the struggling child out of the private school and began anew in another private school. This meant that for the rest of their lives our children would have separate friends, parties to attend, school sports events to cheer at and against, etc. We were young and thought we were doing the right thing, but seeing Jesus through a grandmother's eyes now, I know it was the wrong thing to do. I regret we did not consult other adults as to how to confront the Head Master who was an older man and prided himself on "fund raising."

Teach your children how to stand up for themselves.

Teach your children how unimportant the words are that come out of the mouth of an angry person. Cursing is used in an effort to take authority over someone. If an angry person is trying to take authority over your child in order to build themselves up, help your child see them as someone who is to be pitied. Tomorrow things will change. Practice this with them. Mama used to say, "Sticks and stones may break my bones, but words can never hurt me." Of course, that is easier said than done. Words can hurt you emotionally. This is where our children need help understanding why a person has the need to be hurtful to another person. If your child is mature enough, you might even be able to teach them how to negotiate this argument and bring peace to the situation. Look through obstacles to see your goal.

Laugh often. Show your children it is okay to laugh at themselves. Try not to take yourself so seriously.

Say "Yes," more often!

Love your children in the way they can receive it. Each child is different. Quality time spent with each one individually is you building your best Christ life into their lives.

Write your teenagers a card, a funny card, with a short message of encouragement on it. Slip it under their closed door.

Speak truth to your children while you rock them or at any time you feel you have their attention and the opportunity presents itself.

Hide a cute, sweet, thoughtful note in your little one's lunch or snack box. They will love the surprise when they open the box.

Tell them you love them before they leave the house, or when they get out of the car. Tell them you love them before they go to sleep. Any time is good to tell someone you love them.

Help them when they are frustrated. Get up and support them as they find their solutions. Cheer them on!

Teach them to be nice to everyone. The children who are not in their little group are probably wishing they were. Lots of nerds grow up to be people you wish you had known better while you were in school together.

Feed them a good breakfast. Give them something good to eat right after school. They are hungry. Give them a piece of jelly bread before they brush their teeth to go to sleep. Food in their stomach helps them sleep better.

Eat breakfast and dinner together as a family everyday. You miss so much of your child's opening up and telling you what is on his or her mind if you do not sit together while eating. Be sure the T.V. is turned off!

Pray for your children, and with your children. Talk about answers to prayer, setting before them examples of God's faithfulness.

Hug them as often as is appropriate. We all need that physical, loving touch.

Chapter Six
ALONE WITH GOD

In the year 1979 in early August, Ed and I took our children to Cancun, Mexico, for our summer vacation. We stayed in a Club Med, which was so much fun! The compound was all-inclusive so the children could go to their separate choices of activities and never leave the guarded resort. They were teens and they were safe.

Ed and I took more sailing lessons, windsurfing lessons, and we danced. The meals were delicious, all you could eat of the fresh seafood they caught daily. It was a blast. Brad became certified in scuba diving, we all went snorkeling, and at night, the Club had a nightclub for the teens! They stayed up until 2:30 A.M., having fun with other teens that were there with their parents. Brad had a great time meeting Barbra Streisand's niece and her friends. (I still have a picture I took of her. She looks just like Barbra!) Adelle had a crush on a boy she met who was from Atlanta. (A good trip with teenagers at that time.)

Club Med also offered a side trip to the Mayan Indian Ruins. I was interested, so I signed up to go. Ed stayed behind with the kids. It was an all day trip by bus, with a stop for lunch at a local restaurant. It was 92 degrees outside! The ruins were oppressive. Evil had certainly reigned there in previous years. The guide showed us a wide, round, 200-foot deep pit, filled with dirty green water. He told us this was where, in past times, the Mayan people offered their babies in sacrifice to their gods. (They threw their live children into this pit to die!) All I could do was pray for God to forgive the horrible deaths of these children.

We climbed the pyramids in the heat. They were impressive but the 92-degree weather caused us to become overheated. We were given a bottle of cold beer to drink afterwards. I don't care for beer, but anything cold at that moment sounded refreshing. I was near heat stroke condition; it was that hot. Though an interesting experience, I was glad to return to the Club and enjoy the remainder of our trip.

We completed our vacation and returned to Atlanta. (All this is to tell you how this trip led me to another time alone with God.) Three months later, I developed hepatitis, Type C, the worst kind you can get! My eyeballs were yellow and I was very tired. This is what sent me to Dr. Thorne Winter, my devoted M.D. He put me in the hospital for tests to determine exactly what was going on. They asked me where I had been three months earlier. When I told them Cancun, Mexico, they determined I had contracted this disease through contact with infected bodily fluids. They had no way to determine the exact point of contact. I remembered hugging an old woman the day we went to see the Mayan ruins. She was sick and begging. I held her and told her Jesus loved her and said a little prayer over her. I do not know if her infection might have been on her dirty clothes or some blood, or bodily fluid that somehow infected me.

After the diagnosis, the hospital I was in dismissed me immediately. Hepatitis C is so highly contagious, I was sent home right away.

Dr. Winter ordered me to bed rest for the next two months, informing Ed and me there were no meds to help cure this disease I had contracted. Ed had to take some kind of shots to protect him from becoming infected. God was calling me to His side, once again. All I was able to do for eight weeks was read and sleep. In addition, all I felt like reading was my Bible.

Ed and the children did everything for me, the dogs, the house, grocery shopping, homework, carpool, everything. Thanksgiving and Christmas were coming. (This was bad timing for a mother to be sick!) Adelle was twelve years old now, Brad 14 ½. I will never forget how Adelle practically single handed, pulled off Christmas, selecting and wrapping gifts for everyone. Ed had gotten Christmas dinner together with the help of Morrison's Cafeteria Restaurant, but he forgot to buy rolls. I could hardly believe it when the doorbell rang on Christmas Eve day, there stood my sweet across the street neighbor, Dixie, bringing us beautiful big rolls to add to our Christmas dinner! God is so good. Dixie probably had no way of knowing how specifically those rolls spoke to me. She was used of our Lord in her obedience to buy "rolls," not a ham or potatoes, but the one thing we did not have and needed. I knew God had His hand on our family, but I am not sure I thoroughly understood all He was up to as He continued to build our faith.

All that Adelle accomplished over that Christmas was most unusual for a 12 year old. (She is, to this day, one of the most capable people I know.) Thank you Adelle, sweet daughter of mine!

During the next two months, every day, several times a day, I read my Bible. God's words were sticking in my head without a thought of memorizing. They were just sinking deep into my soul with understanding.

One day Adelle came in my bedroom to tell me something and whatever I said to her, her reply was; "Mom, do you realize that every word that comes out of your mouth these days is scripture?" She wasn't really "put out" with me, but she wanted some Mom time with me. Not Mom and Jesus time.

God was doing a mighty work in my life and I loved it. There was no way I could have been allowed the time to be alone with Jesus like this. The responsibilities any mother has during child rearing years keeps her pretty busy unless Christ pulls her aside.

Once again, my sister came to my rescue. She and my brother-in-law were living in Ft. Lauderdale, Florida, at this time. They purchased beautiful, delicious, huge navel oranges from some orchard near their home and sent me a bag once a week for eight weeks. She was persuaded Vitamin C would get me well.

Ed was faithful to peel these oranges and serve them to me in my bed twice every day. I don't know if the secret is eating the meat of the orange as well as the freshness of the juice, but sure enough, I got well. (Oranges or not, I knew it was Jesus that blessed this effort and used it to heal my body.) Thank you Jesus, for loving me so much.

At the end of the two months bed rest, Dr. Winter drew blood and determined I was one of only 2% of people who ever really get over Hepatitis C. Of course I am not surprised. There is nothing too hard for God. I am not ever allowed to donate blood in the future, but I am persuaded God had once again delivered me from evil.

Being alone with God is such a remarkable experience; you don't ever want it to end. Yes, I missed seeing my children play in their sporting events, etc. and being with my friends, and of course being a wife to Ed. But as my body began to heal and I became aware I was getting stronger and could resume some of my responsibilities, I realized I was not going to have those long seasons of time with Jesus that I had enjoyed during bed rest. It was hard for me to "re-enter" society, if that makes any sense. I had all but been in a cloister with Christ, yet now was being called back into the world.

It was apparent to me the world was shallow. People's conversations were about nothing. Just words came out of their mouths that absolutely had no value. Southerners are good at that thing called manners. We talk all around a subject to pad the way to saying what is really on our minds and think those who don't do this are abrupt!

It was time to come down off the mountaintop. I now had a better understanding of why people decide to become nuns and monks. I experienced re-entry with one eye looking back over my shoulder hoping God would allow me this experience with Him again one day. What Satan had meant for evil, God had used for good.

Experiences like these build your faith in ways that serve you the remainder of your life. God had been so close, so real to me. I knew then, He would never leave me nor forsake me. This gave me the courage to continue on my journey.

Chapter Seven

TEENAGE TO ADULT CHILDREN

Once your child, always your child! It is such a pleasure to have children in your life, whether young or grown. They are, as the scripture calls them, "our rewards." And truly, they are, just as we are a reward to our parents. To see God's repetition of physical likenesses in them, to experience their successes with them, to enjoy their companionship and friendship is like nothing else. Children are God's best illustration of creation. God's favorite of all he created; man.

All this to say be careful how you live, your attitudes and words, your habits and relationships with others. Fathers, you are teaching your sons and daughters how to treat other people in their relationships with their friends, spouses, business partners, as well as how to parent. Every aspect of their lives is being touched each day by your example, either positively or negatively. We are sending signals, messages to them which are being stored away to become a part of who they are. Children soak up information like a sponge. Their learned behavior will become a big part of who they are.

This little story came across the internet one day that illustrates how children soak up information like a sponge.

As the story goes, a wife invited some people to dinner. At the table, she turned to their six-year-old daughter and said, "Would you like to say the blessing?" "I wouldn't know what to say," the girl replied. "Just say what you hear Mommy say," the wife answered. The daughter bowed her head and said, "Lord, why on earth did I invite all these people to dinner?"

Ed and I have a fun memory of an outing he shared with our son, Brad. Each time we talk about it we laugh all over again. Ed was 25 years old; Brad was 2 1/2. They were going to the hardware store this Saturday morning. (Ed took Brad everywhere with him.) There was a bag of fertilizer spread half way on the sidewalk and half falling off the curb. It was obvious the wire around it had broken somehow and the bale was separating. Brad took one look at this mess and as Ed held his little hand helping him up the curb onto the sidewalk, Brad said, "Boy Dad, someone sure kicked the hell out of that, didn't they?"

Ed came home and told me the story. We realized then our son was old enough to know not only what we were saying, but exactly how and when to use curse words. We stopped a bad habit that day. God's opportunity for positive change in our lives!

As one little boy was overheard praying, "Lord, forgive us our trash baskets as we forgive those who put trash in our baskets."

Yes, it is hard to watch a child act out learned behavior. Especially if it is not good behavior and you know they have learned it from you. No matter what age your child, they are always yours. If you have a teenager who is on the road to self-destruction, you as a parent or grandparent should probably seek outside help for the teen. This behavior illustrates them calling out for help, and you have probably already talked yourself blue in the face trying to help them and guide them in the right direction.

Like the little boy who was talking to God, said, "Lord if you can't make me a better boy, don't worry about it. I'm having a real good time like I am." Many children are having so much fun misbehaving with their friends; they have no desire to change. Teens are trying to figure life out, spread their wings and test those hormones that are flying.

Their friends are so important to them. Whichever group accepts them and whomever they feel comfortable with, tells you how they are feeling about themselves. If they choose a girlfriend that doesn't seem to match, perhaps they feel like they do not deserve someone more suitable, successful or well accepted by friends. Parents, be careful to compliment teens as often as is earned. Their self-esteem is still being developed and feelings usually live on the surface during these years.

I recall a pastor telling me one time his son was about to propose to the girl he had dated for a year. She was not very pretty, didn't have a personality and my friend could not understand what his son saw in her. Therefore, he asked him one day when they were talking, "Son, are you physically attracted to your girl?" The son thought for a minute and said, "No." As the conversation continued the pastor discovered his son was settling for this girl because he did not believe he deserved a person like his mother or sister. Let's give this son the name Bill for the sake of communication.

My friend began to have talks with Bill about his own self-image. The thoughts of engagement began to vanish as Bill began to believe who God said he was, rather than who Bill thought others had projected him to be. Several months later Bill found a new relationship developing. This time the girl excited Bill. She was full of personality, came from a great family, loved to be with Bill's family, and seemingly could not say enough nice things about Bill. She obviously adored him, and was thrilled to be with him. He felt loved and appreciated for who he was. A year later they were married and still are today. Had Bill's Dad not helped him see how important he is to God and to his family, and what a special man he is, Bill would have unhappily settled for and married a girl who was not God's best for him.

It is so important to get to know your children's friends. If they will not bring them home, you know something's up. That is unless the child has a bad home environment that will not allow them the freedom to bring friends into the home.

Sometimes embarrassment keeps us from wanting to admit we need help with our children. You really don't want to believe it yourself, so you do nothing. Or you feel helpless and don't know what to do. May I suggest you deal with it now? Later is always harder and depending on what your teen is involved in, there may not be a later. If later does come, and there is no constructive change, there will be a broken heart somewhere.

Asking questions and talking to the parents of your child's friends about teen problems such as sex, drugs, misbehavior that can damage a life forever, most probably will result in great disappointment to you. Some will be in denial; others simply don't want to be involved and will not tell you what they know about your child's behavior. Asking them for help usually results in a waste of time and humiliation. Even longtime friends cannot seem to bare the truth and will often times turn their backs on you. If they do stop allowing their children to participate with your child, try to remember they too are trying to protect their own children. You can try contacting the school, but this too will probably be a dead end. Be true to yourself and tell other parents things you know they would want to know about their child, even if they don't listen to you.

Occasionally one of these children will take his or her own life, or be killed in an automobile accident, or worse yet, accidentally take the life of a friend in an automobile accident. All you can do is grieve with their parents and know that you tried to help by coming to them at some earlier time.

I tell our grandchildren often, how fine they are, how special they are to me and to God. Ed and I do all we know to encourage and instill in children who God says they are. When I hear a Mom or a Dad in the grocery store occasionally telling their child he is bad or "You are just bad!" it breaks my heart. If the one they love and trust tells them they are "bad," the child will probably believe it and act out because of a bad self-image.

God will prove His faithfulness to sustain you when you stay on your knees in prayer. Pray for your children and grandchildren every day. Ask God to put extra angels around them and a hedge of protection around them to keep them from all evil. Ask God to protect them from themselves and to give them a clear mind in order to be able to make good choices for their lives. Ask God to somehow let you know what is going on in their lives if you are worried something isn't right.

Many mothers in this world have become strong prayer warriors because their out-of-control children have taken them to their knees. Matthew 21:22 teaches, "And all things, whatsoever ye shall ask in prayer, believing, ye shall receive."

There are resources available to help you know how to keep your children interested and challenged by things they enjoy. The internet has web sites today that can direct you to an agency or a person or place where you can find the help you need.

One thing Ed and I did early on was to pray for God to give our children just one friend in their school who had the same Christian background they had. Someone close to their age who would stand with them when temptations came and help when it was necessary to say that hard word, "No."

Evil is no respecter of persons. Ed and I knew children from the finest families in Atlanta who, as teenagers, were sexually active, having abortions, doing drugs, selling drugs, drinking excessively, being put in jail, participating in lesbianism and gay lifestyles, and who had taken their own lives. Later in life, as adults, the choices they made as teens still remain as scars on the lives unless they know Christ's forgiveness. Shame comes to a person and does something to them. Often it drives one deeper into sin and the spiral goes out of control, lest you are used of God to guide your son or daughter into truth that will set them free. It can be difficult to find where to draw the line in a person's growth and maturity process. Ask your child how you can help; talk to them no matter what.

The heart is described in Ecclesiastes 8:11 as stubborn and in Jeremiah as deceitful and depraved. Matthew 23:25 speaks of extortion and excess, and in Mark 7:21the heart is the fountainhead of all evil. Hebrews 3:12 teaches the heart is the source of unbelief and covetousness. God's Word has much to say about how desperately every man needs His redemptive love.

Wouldn't it be great if people could forgive each other as God forgives us? Yet for some who participate in evil and do not get caught, they pretend they were never a partaker of the destructive lifestyle of choice. As they put others down in order to build themselves up above their own guilt, they somehow feel entitled to be treated like the sin in their lives never existed. God sees it all, forgives it all, and cleanses us from all unrighteousness. He, who is not guilty, throw the first stone.

It is hard to be around those who remind us of our own sin. In addition, it is hard for the sinner to be around a righteous man who is used of God as a mirror in their life. One of the hardest things there is in this life, is to take a look at ourselves. Matthew 23:25 teaches us, "Woe unto you, scribes and Pharisees, hypocrites! For you make clean the outside of the cup and of the platter, but within you are full of extortion and excess."

In Mark 7:18-23 Christ reproaches the scribes and Pharisees "And He said unto them, Are you so without understanding also? Do you not perceive, that whatsoever thing from without entereth into a man, it cannot defile him; Because it entereth not into his heart, but into his belly, and goeth out into the draught, purging all meats? And he saith, that which cometh out of the man, that defileth the man." V. 21, "For from within, out of the heart of men, proceed evil thoughts, adulteries, fornications, murders." V. 22, "Thefts, covetousness, wickedness, deceit, lasciviousness, an evil eye, blasphemy, pride, foolishness." V. 23, "All these evil things come from within, and defile the man."

In addition, Hebrews 3:12 teaches, "Take heed, brethren, lest there be in any of you an evil heart of unbelief, in departing from the living God."

For those who have paid a high price for your wrong choices, I pray you no longer carry the shame that bound you. I pray your choice to believe God, not man, has set you free to hold your head up high in all humility of what Christ has done for you. That you have come to realize you are free, a beautiful witnesses of Christ's faithfulness to forgive and wash us clean. It takes some time for society to trust you after you break your trust with others. However, God looks on the heart and sees your desire to correct your ways. Other people will line up with who "You" think you are in Christ. So I encourage you in knowing that you have done all you can to pay your debt to society and that is all you can do. Yesterday is over, period. I hope your heart is so healed that as you look at yourself in the mirror you see yourself as Jesus sees you; free to live and laugh and be like Christ. I cheer you on!

It is a good thing when you finally learn that a man has the right and obligation to look down at another man, only when that man needs help to get up from the ground. We have all made mistakes.

Chapter Eight

THE EYE OF GOD

"I will instruct thee and teach thee in the way which thou shalt go: I will guide thee with mine eye."

Psalm 32:8

One night while quietly taking a bath, God and I were talking. I was searching my heart about why I could not find peace. Worry was always present. The mistakes of my life haunted me. God turned my thoughts to something I had not thought of before. I heard him say, "You have not forgiven yourself."

Over that last year or so, I had purposed to ask forgiveness from family members and friends whom I felt I had offended in some way. I had asked Ed and the children to forgive me for my shortcomings. Everyone was accepting of my effort and need to ask his or her forgiveness. I was feeling pretty good about this. However, forgiving myself had been something that seemed nondeserving, uncomfortable in some foreign respect. I could not restore my own heart. My feelings were still too stuck.

No one had ever talked to me about a need to line up a feeling with a memory, but I heard God's voice saying, "I see a heart that is broken and sincere; one truly sorry for things you have done and cannot take back. This is why I came and died on the Cross for you, Joanne. Is that not enough?" "Your memories have feelings that long to heal, but I cannot heal you without your permission. Your thoughts need to be transformed by my shed blood. Forgiveness is for you, not for the other fellow. When you forgive, you stand right with me because I have given my all so that you can be forgiven. Furthermore, I have commanded you to forgive and that means forgiving yourself as well as others. Remember my commandment to forgive others as I have forgiven you?" God's small voice continued in my head and heart; "If I have forgiven you, who are you not to forgive yourself?" "You have done all you can to be forgiven, except you have not received my sacrifice for your sins. Your disobedience is holding you prisoner in your own heart and that is not pleasing to me."

I started crying because I knew this was truth, God's truth that would set me free. My unforgiveness of myself was holding me back; robbing, stealing and destroying relationships and accomplishments. In that moment, a light bulb turned on in my heart and head. The truth of my disobedience and arrogance and self-serving indulgence to even think I needed to add something to what Jesus had already done for me, made me feel sick.

A fast rewind of my thoughts flooded my mind. Everything I knew about forgiveness filled my heart. How had I been able to help others enter into God's forgiveness? Was I so blind as not to be able to see my own mistakes! It is sickening when you are finally ready to let God show you your own self. My self-righteousness was as filthy rags like Isaiah had said. How could I have been so long rejecting the sacrificial lamb that I loved? God's eye had guided me and taught me because I was ready; I was tired of carrying a need for an excuse for my behavior. I longed for my relationships to be restored and that meant with Christ as well as with others.

Something inside of me felt like a back to the future ride. Almost instantly, God removed the raw feelings from my heart that had been giving me excuses to hold onto disconnected relationships like the one I had with Mama and wanted so desperately to have restored. I had many times expressed my forgiveness of Mama to the Lord, but the ill feelings over that stupid hairbrush day would not go away. Part of me was glad and part of me was sad. On the days that I really wanted to be close to Mama, I was sad something was holding me back. And on the days when Mama aggravated me, I had my excuse for being angry with her and had no problem telling her so!

Seeing my unforgiveness through God's eyes was a whole new matter. God's eyes have been upon me all of my life, and now He had given me the ability to see my life "through" His eyes. I was not willing to disagree with God about His love and grace towards me any longer. In an instant, yesterday was gone. Yesterday was Over! I had finally come to the END of my ignorance in this area of my life.

It did not take me long to realize this new way of thinking was going to "cost" me. A new beginning had begun. I now knew when I got aggravated in the future I was going to have to be responsible for my words and actions. No more excuses about the hairbrush day. Now what I had to say to Ed and the children would be out of a fresh place, out of a forgiven heart and soul. It took some time for my feelings to catch up with the truth God had shown me. But in time, they were exchanged for the reminder of "Who" God is in my life and all that He has done to provide forgiveness for me. He is well able to be and to do in and through me, as well as apart from me! Because I now felt God's forgiveness of me, my heart and thoughts gave me new eyes to see not only myself, but others as well. Life felt free. It felt right and good. I knew this was Jesus.

To trust that God is healing those I have hurt is my only choice now. The memory of the sorrow I caused myself empowers me to see life through mistakes and failures, giving me wisdom to guide and suggest through a grandmother's eyes of experience. The hard part is we cannot pass down our lessons learned in life. We cannot give them to our children and grandchildren except through our example. They too must come to Christ as little children, humbling themselves before Jesus and ask Him for forgiveness of their own sins. If we could keep them from their sins, save them from the pain of failures, they probably would not find their need for Christ. God has an order to His creation, and I am so desperately grateful He does.

1 Samuel 15:23 says, "Behold, to obey is better than sacrifice, and to harken than the fat of rams. For rebellion is as the sin of witchcraft, and stubbornness is as iniquity and idolatry." My stubborn "will" had brought pain and evil into my life and I wanted no further part in it.

As a child, I loved curling up in my Daddy's lap, and now I had that freedom again, to curl up with my heavenly Father and just be. What had stood in between my heart and God had vanished that night in the bathtub! I could almost see my sin going down the drain when I unplugged it, letting the dirty water out.

Once in a while, our grandchildren quietly join us on the sofa as we are watching something on T.V. They kind of slide their body up under our arms without saying a word and just sit there. No words are spoken; we simply exchange the warmth of our bodies, sharing the comfort and unspoken love. This is how Jesus desires we come unto Him, as little children. He longs for us to simply curl up with Him and be and exchange and listen and love. This is my heart's song, to come to Christ, to be with Him and listen and learn and love and Be, for His glory. For His glory as I pass along to others the love of Christ, when and however He allows.

One of the rewards of being a grandmother is having the experiences of having been a child, plus the experiences of being a mother, plus the experiences as a grandparent. I believe wisdom is built in our relationship with Christ, our experiences and the opportunities they offer to teach us over and over again, as little children.

I still enjoy some of my best pondering in the bathtub. What is it about water that brings such comfort and freedom to just "Be." I cannot prove it, but I enjoy the suggestion that it is because we are standing naked and unashamed before the Lord. And like when we were encompassed by the water in our mother's womb, we feel safe and comforted. The world is not intruding and we can just get lost in our thoughts of Jesus and His goodness.

Chapter Nine

SETTING AN EXAMPLE OPENING OF THE CHRISTIAN EMBASSY IN WASHINGTON, D.C.

Life is so full of wonderful surprises, yet there is no way to share all of mine with you. I will say being invited to help cater the opening of the Christian Embassy in Washington, D. C., was one of the nicest I can remember.

Campus Crusade for Christ, under the leadership of Bill and Vonett Bright, decided to be a bright witness for Christ in our nation's Capitol in a way that had not been done before. In Washington, there are beautiful homes along a street named Embassy Row. Bill and Vonett acquired one of these homes and celebrated its opening by inviting many of Washington's dignitaries to luncheons and dinner parties where the Gospel of Jesus Christ was presented.

Christian Senators and Congressmen were asked to give their testimonies of how Christ had become such an important part of their lives. Strom Thurman, Chuck Colson and Dr. Charles Stanley, Bill Bright and others were included in the list of speakers. Mary and Claude Brown were there and Cecil and Deen Day attended from Atlanta, Georgia, as well as others from Texas and other states. (I did not know everyones' names who were present.)

Mr. and Mrs. Bright entertained these people in the most beautiful way they knew how. Sterling silver was borrowed and brought from Atlanta. Two very large silver swans were used as the centerpiece on a very long dining room table. They were filled to overflowing with strawberries and all kinds of delicious fruits. We prepared tea sandwiches, cheese and grape platters, homemade breads, cookies, chicken salad, ham, cakes, pies, beautiful vegetables, meats, casseroles, everything you could think of. (Yes, this was a lot of very hard work, but when God has His hand on what you are doing, your work is made easy.) We had so much fun in the kitchen. There was just a general excitement in the air.

The lace tablecloths, flowers and beautiful architecture of the room, brought Southern beauty, grace, and style into this home being used for the Lord. God had anointed us in the kitchen, making every bite of food we prepared delicious and appetizing. We simply were doing what God had taught us to do many times before in our own kitchens, but the glory God brought to this event was amazing.

The Sunday edition of the Washington Post Newspaper that week reported the event and was headlined with the words, "Washington Has Never Seen Anything Like This!" Some of the guests heard the Gospel presented for the first time while others prayed to receive Christ as their Lord and Savior. Lives were changed, never to be the same again. Bill's and Vonett's vision was truly blessed of God and made an impact on our Nations Capitol that only eternity will reveal. God was good; we will never forget the gratitude we felt as we knew His Spirit had been there present among us.

I did not realize God was leading me into a season of catering. Watch out what you pray for.

Earlier that year, I had met a missionary my heart felt led to financially support. The problem was Ed and I did not have any extra money. Therefore, I prayed and asked God to show me how I could earn some extra money without having to leave our home. Our children needed my attention.

After receiving so much encouragement in Washington, I decided to make the recipes that were mine, and were so enjoyed during the occasions we catered and sell them. I told my friends, neighbors,

Church, everyone I came in contact with, that I was starting a catering business to help earn money for my missionary friend. Soon my little business took flight.

The phone began to ring for Jesus! For Jesus, because I gave every dime I earned to the missionary friend and other Church related ministries. One day while in Ogletrees Grocery Store, (a privately owned small chain of stores), Mr. Ogletree was standing there and I had the where-with-all to ask Mr. Ogletree if he would buy the pies I was making. He asked me to bring one in for him to sample. It was at this juncture Ed advised me I best get a Permit from the City to prepare food in my home to be sold in a public place.

I telephoned my friend and Attorney, Bill Frantz. Bill helped prepare the necessary documents and the process began. I received a phone call not too long after Bill filed my request from a representative of the Food and Drug Administration who wanted to come out and check my home kitchen. So we made a date! I cleaned as well as I knew how in anticipation of this man's visit. I really wanted him to like what he saw.

I have forgotten this gentleman's name, I am sorry to say, but the day he arrived, I invited him in to look over my kitchen. While he was looking around and inspecting my kitchen, he began to question me about why and what and who I wanted to cook for. I told him of my missionary friend and before I knew it, I heard myself witnessing to this man. Jesus had arranged a divine appointment for this gentleman and I had not realized it until that very moment. Soon I became aware the man was really listening to me, so I invited him into the living room to sit down. None to my surprise, he bowed his head and joined me in a Prayer of Salvation. This man had prayed to receive Christ as his Lord and Savior right there on the sofa in my living room.

Only one week later, Bill Frantz phoned me. I heard Bill say, "Joanne, you are not going to believe this, but you have been approved by the Food and Drug Administration." "I can hardly believe this myself…," Bill continued. "I have been trying for months to get several of my other clients this same approval and have not gotten it yet. How did you do this?"

I told Bill what had gone on the day of my kitchen inspection and I heard a soft chuckle. Bill said, "Joanne, you are something else." I responded and said, "No, Bill, Jesus is something else!" Without one ounce of foreknowing on my part, God had seen fit to draw one man to Himself as Savior, as well as to be a witness to another man who already knew Christ, and all while I am just hoping my kitchen will pass inspection! I walked around gratefully smiling, all day. This beautiful illustration of God's faithfulness had made my joy full.

I had such fun teaching our children how to make melon balls, cookies and pies. We all had a wonderful time learning a new way to help people and to serve our Lord. The children learned the importance of tithing through this ministry, as well as the value of prayer. God longs to bless us, and He did.

Brad was such a help during all this catering season. He carried endless containers of heavy things to and from my car and never complained. Thank you Brad, you helped your mother as well as participated in an activity that brought honor to our King! We won't know until we get to heaven what good work our missionary friend was able to do with the contributions God allowed us to make in her life.

Second from left, Vonette Bright, Third from left, Joanne Forrest Nutting
Preparing for the Opening of the Christian Embassy, Washington, D.C.

Chapter Ten

PLANTING A SEED

Being Present With God

Jeremiah 5:22, "Fear ye not me? saith the Lord: will ye not tremble at my presence, which have placed the sand for the bound of the sea by a perpetual decree, that it cannot pass it: and though the waves thereof toss themselves, yet can they not prevail; though they roar, yet can they not pass over it?"

The power of the sea has always kept me in awe of Holy God. If you have ever gone sailing, you learn quickly to respect the power of the sea. When I visit the seashore it draws me into the presence of God somehow. Like so many others, my soul and body are restored at the seashore; I love the sounds, the salt and the sand. I find peace in God's creation called the seashore.

Laughter is medicine for the soul. It is so much fun to laugh and play and let your mind and spirit run free at the beach. Sometimes when I feel I need to release tension, I get out the artist's easel. Those big, really big tablets of paper work well or a canvas for acrylics is great if you have the desire. Whichever one I use, I draw big, long lines with energy. A huge eye or a huge heart or the ocean, a tree, whatever comes, then I fill in colors or meaning or a scripture verse. I allow my creative juices to flow no matter what it looks like. The only value it has is the fun and release of pent up energy. You may surprise yourself. Now and then I surprise myself.

God has blessed me with three very close friends who occasionally come to see me at the seashore. We share scriptures and insights, wisdom and prayers, and beautiful music. And we draw! Usually we draw at the end of our fellowship time and the drawings illustrate what God has just shown us. It feels so good to put on paper an expression of what is in our hearts and minds, while being respectfully quiet as the other person draws. When we are all finished drawing, we share the message behind the drawing. These messages are often profound, often life changing. Some would call these moments an epiphany. I call them God's voice and truth leading us on.

The result of seeking is finding; this is what happens during our moments together. It seems like only moments, although in reality hours pass. The friends I am referring to have been sharing with me like this for some nineteen years or so. (Not always drawing.) We still cannot get enough of these times of being together, present with God. It is as though God's power is increased as His truths flow through the four of us. We are very aware God has pulled us aside as well as kept us together for his purposes. God's purposes are bigger than we are; His thoughts are higher than our thoughts and we know He is in the midst of us. It is like having cataract surgery, the doctor telling you it is imperative you hold very still while he is removing the cloud that is impairing your vision. We hear God's voice telling us to be still and know that He is God, to be still and listen to His Spirit within us, because He is about to show us something. He is about to give us wisdom that we've never been able to see before. He is going to take away our blindness and give us His eyes to understand with. We are so blessed during these times of pondering. You can feel the Holy Spirit covering over us. A sense of knowing God is present.

"The righteous cry out, and the Lord hears them; he delivers them from all their troubles." (Psalms 34:17, Thompson Chain Reference Bible, King James Version) The Lord may not deliver us at that moment, but He allows us to see the issue at hand, through His eyes. He gives us new understanding of ourselves and our circumstances which then brings clarity to trust Him as we wait to hear His small still voice, in his perfect timing of illumination and resolve. The picture of "God's Eye" taken by NASA's Hubble Space Telescope was featured on NASA's website as an Astronomy Picture of the Day, May 2003. Though NASA calls it "The Helix Nebula" someone there named it "The eye of God." This photograph had such an impact on my heart when I first saw it the day it came across the internet to me in an email, it took my breath away. It struck me so deep in my spirit I could only look at it for short seconds at the time, and then I would have to turn away as I found I could hardly breathe. At the time, I had no idea how God would continue to use this photograph in my life.

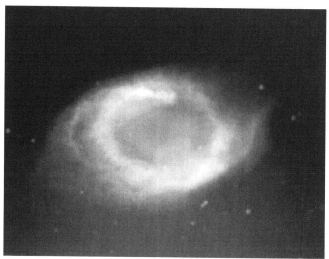

The Eye of God

Schedules and requirements on my life and my friend's lives interfere with our ability to meet with each other, sometimes for

96

months at a time. We live long distances apart. Today as I sit and write, our group had planned to meet, however God sent us sleet and snow! (We were in Atlanta, Georgia.) Therefore, we knew it was not His perfect timing for our meeting. We put one foot in front of the next and make an alternate plan for a different day. We all seem to accept the steps God orders for our group.

We named our group "The Seekers" nineteen years ago after attending a Christian women's retreat together where the scripture chosen for that weekend was, "Seek ye first the kingdom of God, and his righteousness; and all these things shall be added unto you." (Matthew 6:33, King James, Thompson Chain Reference Bible) The objective of the retreat was to teach us, through life experiences of others, how to seek after the heart of God. The retreat is called Tres Dias, which means "Three Days" in Spanish. We had not known each other previous to this meeting and did not have any idea of God's purposes when we arrived there. We see more clearly today a deeper reason why we attended the retreat. In retrospect, we all agreed, you never know what God is up to. Today, when God tells us to go, we stop our lives and go.

(Tres Dias refers to these times of "reuniting" as I do with these women, as "Reunion Groups." The women (or men) who make up these groups are referred to as Reunion Sisters, or Reunion Brothers.)

When the four of us are apart from each other, which is 99% of the time, we live out our individual journey just as we do when we are together, one heart seeking Christ where ever He has put us. Picking up our cross daily, working out what God has put within us, with laughter, and sometimes with tears. This is God's given assignment to each of us. Our common denominator, our common purpose unites us. If we were not all individually seeking the same person of Jesus Christ, our paths would have taken and still would take different directions. We have come to love each other and each other's families; yet we love Jesus more.

You too can invest your life in a friend's life, like my friend Jackie invested her life in mine taking me to Bible study for three years! Seek out that person you can help in whatever way God has given you. Everyone has the need of a loving friend. And by all means, give that artwork a try!

L – R. Barbara, Forrest, Angie, Chris

Chapter Eleven
GOD'S FAITHFULNESS

"The eyes of the Lord are in every place, beholding the evil and the good." Proverbs 15:3

If God has called you to a task, He will keep you while doing the task. Answering the call of God on your life comes with the awareness that the task may not be easy. For you young people who are trying to put one foot in front of the other on your journey, you can know evil hates it when you reach out to others, in the name of Jesus. People are people, Christians, or otherwise, wherever they are on their journey. The flesh can be jealous and selfish, which invites evil to get a toe hole in the door of your life. Let me give you an example.

In July 1996, I was called of God to be Rector of the Tres Dias Christian Women's Retreat in Moscow, Russia. (This is the same kind of retreat where I met my friends that I referred to in Chapter

Ten, as my "Reunion" sisters.) The Tres Dias communities that sponsor these retreats are all over the United States, as well as in other countries. When a new community desires to start a Tres Dias Retreat, they require help getting the experience needed to do so. People who have experience in attending these retreats are called upon to go into other communities to help train and prepare the local fellowship of believers how to hold their own retreats. (Each retreat has a leader and team members. Each time the retreat has a different leader. The leader is called the Rector.)

So I am now being called to lead this new community in their Retreat, along with approximately fifty other volunteers from across the United States, all having had experience participating in Tres Dias retreats in their hometowns.

Each volunteer going to Moscow for this retreat paid his or her own way as well as donated an equal amount so that a Russian man or woman could attend as a guest. We would be in Moscow for two weeks.

When the Representative of the International Tres Dias Community called me and invited me to be the leader for this retreat, I was humbled and grateful, but knew I could only be there for the one week of the ladies retreat. I could not be there for the first week during which time the men's retreat would be held. They wanted me to be the Rector no matter what excuse I gave them, so off I went. God was calling me and I knew He would keep me in His care.

(Hang in here with me as I get to the illustration of how evil is present in the selfishness of mankind.)   When the plane landed in Moscow, I looked out the window and saw military men dressed in camouflage uniforms carrying automatic weapons! I had never seen this before. They were present throughout the airport, so I was somewhat relieved when I was greeted by the Men's Leader and a driver who safely took me to the campground where the meeting was to be held.

The first item of business was to have a gathering with all the women and pastors who would be serving on the retreat. All of these volunteers had already been there for a week serving during the Men's Retreat, and had experienced a sweet time of bonding as they watched God change Russian men's lives, giving them the hope that only Christ can give. Everyone's sacrifice had been blessed in a mighty way. You simply cannot out give God; the more the American men gave to the Russian men, the more God gave back to them. No one even noticed how hard their circumstances were.

That evening we all gathered together and, as Rector, I called the meeting to order. Every team member was there. After greeting everyone and telling them how happy I was to be there, I saw one of the ladies raise her hand. As I finished expressing my desire to get started fulfilling our duties, I called on the lady that had her hand up, giving her permission to speak. She introduced herself to me as Kay.

Her flesh got the best of her and out of her mouth came the words, "Why are you the Rector? We have already been here serving the men's team for a week, visiting orphanages, not getting enough to eat, sleeping on army cots from World War 1 with roaches crawling over us, and you haven't done a thing!"

Another lady raised her hand and continued to insinuate she was as qualified as I was, etc. More verbal abuse proceeded out of her mouth. Jealousy and hunger and signs of fatigue and totally being out of their comfort zone had their flesh flying! They were on their last nerve. (Remember, these are Godly women we are talking about.)

After what seemed like a long meeting of trying to be gracious and ask their forgiveness for my absence, and on and on, I felt tears begin to warm my cheeks. Nothing I said seemed to bring peace to the meeting. I decided to bring the meeting to a close and start over the next day. We were all tired. At that moment, the three pastors approached me, one of them speaking to all the ladies saying, "Forrest is the Rector of this retreat because God has called her to be the Rector." And with that, the pastors began to wash my feet and pray over me. The room became so quiet you could almost hear my tears drop. I will always be marked by the Holy Spirit awareness and obedience of my friend Pastor David Grubbs, as well as the other two pastors who washed my feet. (Pastor Grubbs is pastor of a church in Duluth, Georgia, who traveled to Moscow with our group.)

The following day we toured the retreat site. The head pastor stayed right beside me. This was most comforting. It did not take long to realize this facility was filthy and our team would have to clean it before the retreat began. I remember going to the husband of the lady who was assigned to clean the rest rooms and asking his permission for her to do this. I knew in my heart she would be at risk for contracting a disease. Her husband gave me his permission to allow her to clean as a true servant would. We were shown to the Chapel where I was to lead a short time of prayer and thanksgiving for the facility, the members of our group, and our guests who were to attend the retreat. Each group would be given their service area locations.

After touring the facility I took time to visit each group to be sure things were going smoothly and to see what the areas of need were.

As I walked into the service area called the "Palanca" Room (small gifts, a lever of love) I noticed big plastic boxes stacked from floor to ceiling. Each box was filled to the brim with things to be used on the weekend that needed to be unpacked, organized and put in the appropriate place. There were probably forty or fifty of these large boxes. The lady who was in charge of Palanca was not there. I asked, "Where is Kay?" They answered, "Kay is so overwhelmed she is crying. The Pastors have taken her to the Chapel for prayer."

This was not funny, but paradoxical. God had seen fit to humble this arrogant lady who thought she could handle leading the whole retreat, by showing her she was going to need His help just handling the one area she had been assigned. Kay's flesh had been publicly "out there." It was not hard to be reminded I had better be on the watch for my own.

Over the three days of the Retreat, God's powerful loving, mighty hand, through the voice of a translator for every word I spoke, began to bring hope and change in the Russian women's lives. These women were so precious, grateful, talented, and hungry to know more of Christ. They had nothing, but gave so very much. (Several of them left the Retreat during one of the breaks, which you are not supposed to do. They got on a bus and rode to somewhere, purchased a small golden colored, glass cup and saucer, and brought it back to me as a gift. From Russia, with love; this cup and saucer remain among my most treasured possessions.) God had restored these beautiful women's hope and loved them as only He can. Their lives would never be the same. As they received the teaching and were given the tools that I have tried to give you in this book, to seek and find the intimate relationship with Christ that brings freedom and joy to your inner life, they could now go home and sit at the feet of Jesus and do the work of working out their own salvation, no matter what they had to face in their tomorrows.

My life too, was changed. I truly had new eyes to see how powerful God's presence and love are, in the lives of women who don't even have enough food to eat. This experience of a lifetime had put a mark on my heart forever. I cried tears of thanksgiving and gratitude the whole way back to Atlanta (some eight hours). After I got home, every time I turned on the faucet and had running water that was clean enough to drink, I cried. When I went to bed at night I praised Jesus there were no roaches on the walls. Even when I approached the refrigerator, my heart was filled with gratitude as the women in Russia had no refrigeration. When I drove my car, I thought of them and still do. Women are not allowed to have a Drivers License unless they are a mechanic. There was no one to call if your car broke down. There are so many things we take for granted as Americans. God has truly blessed America. I wish every American could experience a mission type trip like this trip. I understand now why some of our soldiers kiss the ground when they return to the great United States of America.

For months after, in my prayers and reflections I could recall the looks of defeat on the Russian women's faces, looks that had turned to joy even if only temporarily. As their faces shone, you could see the beauty of God's love. I continue to pray for them, even as I write.

The experiences the Tres Dias Communities in the United States and Russia, have provided me, have enriched my life in ways that I could never have imagined when I was a young woman struggling. As I put one foot forward and made myself put action to following Christ, He took me by the hand and made my challenges understandable and peaceful. Tres Dias has been used of my Lord Jesus to give me opportunity to learn how to lead other women into the saving grace of God. Through each work experience as I served in different areas of the retreats for over twenty-five years or so, I have overcome my fear of praying out loud, speaking in front of a crowd of people, and taking on bigger and harder areas of responsibility. With each step God blessed my life and grew me up in Him. I found I am no longer a child, but a grandmother who still comes to Jesus as a little child. It has been my privilege and joy to direct others in how to find Christ and how to walk in the presence of God's eye. Thank you Tres Dias Communities for being used of God to love me in this way.

May God continue to keep His hand on this wonderful effort, and to those of you participating in Tres Dias today, I encourage you to serve every opportunity God calls you to do so. Listen and learn and pray as you go. The blessing will be all yours, as you bless the lives of those who are coming after you. And for anyone who would like to attend a Tres Dias Retreat, just go to the Tres Dias web site on the internet and make your request. God will do the rest.

Chapter Twelve

THE COMFORTER HAS COME

(This Chapter is kind of heavy. Therefore, you will need to hang in here with me as you read. You might get a cold drink, and pick your favorite chair to sit in before you begin. These are life changing truths, so let's get started!)

God, The Holy Spirit, the Comforter, lives inside of every believer's spirit.

John 16:7-14; "Nevertheless I tell you the truth; it is expedient for you that I go away: for if I go not away, the Comforter will not come unto you; but if I depart, I will send him unto you. And when he is come, he will convince the world of its sin, and of the availability of God's goodness, and of deliverance from judgment. The worlds' sin is unbelief in me; there is righteousness available because I go to my Father, and you shall see me no more; there is deliverance from judgment because the prince of this world has already been judged. I have yet many things to say unto you, but you cannot bear them now. Howbeit when he, the Spirit of truth is come, he will guide you into all truth: for he shall not speak of himself; but whatsoever he shall hear, that shall he speak: and he will shew you things to come. He shall glorify me: for he shall receive of mine, and shall shew it unto you."

Do you know, when you prayed the prayer of salvation and invited Jesus into your heart, and asked him to forgive you of your sins, He not only came into your life and forgave you of your sins, but He sent the Comforter, God's Holy Spirit, to indwell your spirit. God's Holy Spirit now lives in you for the purpose of teaching you and telling you the things of God that He would have you understand. Christ gave you an open line of communication from your spirit straight to Holy God! And Holy God now has a way to speak directly to His Spirit, which dwells in you. Then His Spirit tells you all the things that God desires to tell you; just as John 16 teaches us He will.

This is one of the most profound parts of The Gospel any man can grasp. When you truly understand the function and the unction of God's Holy Spirit in you, you understand how to hear God's voice. In addition, being able to hear God's voice, guiding you into all truth, is the key to every man's relationship with Christ. "My sheep hear my voice, and I know them, and they follow me." (John 10:27)

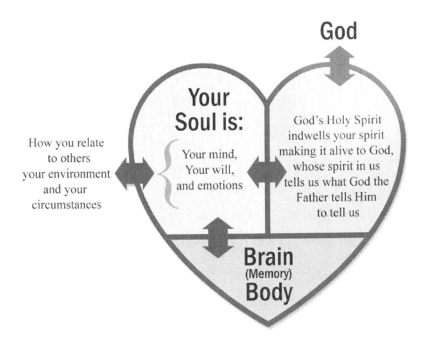

We are created in God's image, a three part being. God is Father, Son and Holy Spirit. We are Spirit, Soul and Body.

After we receive Christ as our Savior, our sinful separation from God is forgiven by Christ's death. Our sins have been paid for in full, by the shed blood of Christ, positionally and conditionally. We are no longer separated from God.

Let me explain. There are two aspects of salvation. One is our positional separation from God, and two is the condition of the sinful heart. Because Adam sinned in the Garden of Eden, his sin separated him from Holy God. As Adam's ancestor, we are born positionally separated from God. Thus we have a need for the blood payment through Christ's death, (and resurrection) for the forgiveness of our ancestral sins. Our ancestral sins placed us in the position of having a need to be restored to the "position" of no longer being separated from God.

The second aspect of salvation is the sinful condition of the heart. Thus, we have a need for Christ's death payment on the Cross for our learned, willful behavior that does not line up with God's Word. We make sinful choices out of ignorance or out of our old belief system stored in our brain which has not yet been renewed. Our brains have not yet exchanged wrong information for God's Word, which is the truth that sets us free from all unrighteousness. As we make choices relying on what is in our memory bank, apart from Christ, often we sin. Christ's death on the Cross is payment in our stead, for all of our past, present and future sins. Please hear me say, God's forgiveness is not meant to be a license to freely sin.

As we see God's grace now flowing through our lives as believers, we see God's forgiveness is for us, not the person who offended us. The pain we bring upon ourselves when we sin grieves God because it scars our lives. We sow and we reap, and we reap longer than we sow. We are accountable though forgiven.

John 1:12, 3:3, "But as many as received him, to them gave he power to become the sons of God, even to them that believe on his name."

Jesus answered and said unto him, "Verily Verily I say unto you, except a man be born again, he cannot see the kingdom of God." (John 3:3)

Romans 10:13 teaches us; "For whosoever shall call upon the name of the Lord shall be saved."
In addition, I Corinthians 1:30 teaches, "But of him are you in Christ Jesus, who of God is made unto us wisdom, and righteousness, and sanctification, and redemption."

As we see that IN CHRIST we have entered into a New Life, as a new creature being born again, and that In Christ because He has always been and always will be, and because as believers in Christ, we are spiritually joined with Him in His eternal time line, we must examine the word eternal. By definition, eternal indicates no beginning or end. It exceeds the boundaries of time. Since Christ is God, He has always lived and always will. His life is the same yesterday, today and forever. (Hebrews 13:8) As portrayed at the beginning of time, In God, Christ "became flesh" (John 1:14) and lived in a human body for some 33 years. Then, He was crucified, buried and raised from the dead on the third day. (1Cor. 15.3:4) He continues to live today. (Hebrews 7:25) Note that eternal life is not only a present and future reality for the believer, but also involves the eternal past because Christ, In God, always was. We will live IN CHRIST throughout eternity, seated at the right hand of God, because God said so in His Word.

Ephesians 1:4 teaches; "According as he hath chosen us in him before the foundation of the world, that we should be holy and without blame before him in love:" Hebrews 13:8 teaches, "Jesus Christ the same yesterday, and today, and for ever." (King James, Thompson Chain Reference) He chose to make provision for us before the foundation of the world. That is why God in his omnipresence (ability to be present everywhere at the same time), knew He needed to be a three part bring. (The Holy Trinity)

Christ always was, and always will be. And IN HIM, spiritually, we too always were, and always will be. We come from God the Creator, and return to God the Creator in Spirit form, in Christ.

Christians now have the hope, given by Christ, for eternal life. The provision has been made for believers to live a new life forgiven on this earth, as well as a spirit life after death in eternity IN CHRIST. The resurrected life transforms us from being a life separated from God and unable to hear His voice (some call it being dead to God), to a life which is alive to God in our spirits, indwelled by God's

Holy Spirit. The resurrected life in eternity, after God calls us to Himself in death, is promised to all believers.

So now, we find our spirit is quickened to the voice of God. We can hear Him within the quietness of our minds and hearts. It is an internal hearing, a hearing that comes with a knowing. A knowing that the still, small voice that is like no other is God speaking to us.

In addition, because God chose not to "Make" us love Him as though we were a puppet, He gave us a free Will. He gave us a choice maker that belongs to each individual, no one else. We are all free to make our individual decisions. We also have emotions individual emotions that allow us to feel and sense for our protection and pleasure; to love and hate, and relate to others.

And of course, God gave us a mind. Our minds are so powerfully created by God they rule our being. The mind functions in synchronization with the emotions, will and the brain (where your memory bank of life experiences is stored). Our habit is to pull up information from our memory bank, which may or may not be transformed. We must form a new habit of communicating with the Holy Spirit in us, seeking God's mind for our lives as we read our Bible and get to know God. It is the Holy Spirit's job to listen to God and to tell us what God tells him to tell us. Then we are to reach down into our memory bank and compare what is stored in our memory, with the truth of God's Word. God never falls down on His job; He never leaves us nor forsakes us. God is available at all times to help us sort out what is in us that is not of Him, as well as help us with the emotion that is attached to the memory. God longs to bring His love and healing to replace the pain in our hearts and minds. His truth is powerful and trustworthy.

Your free Will agrees with God, but there is something within every person called "obstinacy and perversity." Sin is a perverse disposition which entered into man. If you do not know Christ, you are left out there on your own to make your decisions and choices apart from God's voice. Moreover, if you do know Christ and you choose to quench, or turn your thoughts away from God's Holy Spirit speaking to you, you are walking in your own obstinacy, left to do the best you can with what you have programmed into your memory bank.

In a born again or regenerated person, the source of the Will is God, the Almighty. "For it is God which worketh in you, both to will and to do of his good pleasure." (Philippians 2:13) We work out what God works in, not work what you might call "your own salvation," trying to earn your way to Christ's forgiveness. God is the source of your will. Obstinacy is an unintelligent "wage" that refuses to be enlightened. Obedience to the Holy Spirit in you is the only solution to obstinacy.

Let me say this again: As your mind reaches down into your memory bank and pulls up an old thought that has not been transformed by God's truth, you are left to choose from whatever the world or your experiences have led you to believe. Each failure, each hard lesson learned, each time you hurt someone, each time you say something you wish you could take back, can now become either a failure, or an opportunity. As I experienced in my bathtub that night, we have a choice, a failure to learn from God only to repeat sin again, or an opportunity to exchange our old way of thinking and believing for God's truth as written in the Bible. If you choose to block God's voice in your inner being, you will repeat this experience again, over and over, until you decide to listen to God. When you become ready and willing to turn and reach out and again hold hands with God's Holy Spirit, He is forever standing ready and willing to reach for your hand. God longs to have fellowship with you. When we quench God's Holy Spirit, we grieve God. When we make wrong choices because we are stubborn, obstinate, and hurt ourselves, we grieve God. He longs to give us the desires of our hearts, yet is forced by our sinful unintelligent wage to withhold His blessings from us when we don't listen and follow His Holy Spirit truth. As long as we are stubborn and rebellious, it is not good that God bless us. We would get a wrong message and think God is blessing our sin. Would you bless your child for his sin? It would not be good for them, would it? We must give God permission to settle our unintelligent wages.

Here is another hard truth. (I have talked about this scripture verse in another Chapter, but feel it is worthy to mention twice.) I Samuel 15:23, "Behold, to obey is better than sacrifice, and to listen than the fat of rams. For rebellion is as the sin of witchcraft, and stubbornness is as iniquity and idolatry."

When we are stubborn, I Samuel teaches us our stubbornness or obstinacy is likened to iniquity and idolatry. Therefore, we then are sinning by idolizing our thoughts and ways above God's. We become as little Gods within our evil heart. And, I Samuel 15 goes on to teach us that when we are rebellious, it is as though we are participating in witchcraft.

Witchcraft is what Satan is waiting for us to open up to so he can jump right in our minds and misguide us into our own lies that tell us we have a right to our obstinacy. Satan cannot touch us lest we let him. However, when we open the door through sinful beliefs, we invite evil in. Satan becomes our cheerleader for failure. God holds us responsible for our rebelliousness, because He loves us. He has to wait for us to agree with Him. Wait for us to choose the truth that will set us free from our old ways and thoughts. Our old habits eclipse God's truths until we form the new habit of reaching, listening, and learning from God. Our environments need to be changed often times, as they drag us back into our old ways. We need new learning experiences, new friends who have our same goals to know Christ. We need people around us who will encourage us in our new life in Christ. When we are free, we are free indeed; God, then, is free to give us His richest blessings.

"Blessed is the man that walketh not in the counsel of the ungodly, nor standeth in the way of sinners, nor sitteth in the seat of the scornful. But his delight is in the law of the Lord; and in his law doth he meditate day and night. And he shall be like a tree planted by the rivers of water, that bringeth forth his fruit in his season; his leaf also shall not wither; and whatsoever he doeth shall prosper." (Psalms 1:1-3)

I believe God rejoices each time we are enlightened to His truth. When we get tired of needing our excuses to blame others, He is right there ready to set us free. I believe He smiles down on us and cannot wait to love us, heal us, nurture us, hold us and bless us in each and every opportunity. Our failures do not have to be repeated if we will only listen to God. Remember, I previously talked about facing ourselves as being the hardest thing we will ever do. Many people choose never to grow up in Christ, never to be conformed to His image, only to waste all of God's bountiful plans for one's life. Do we really want to miss God's bounty for our lives? God is waiting for us to come to Him. Remember, He did not make us as a puppet.

Also remember, each believer holds a position in God's life, the position of being in Christ. John 17:21 teaches, "That they all may be one; as thou, Father, art in me, and I in thee, that they also may be one in us: that the world may believe that thou hast sent me."

Ephesians 2:6 teaches, "And he hath raised us up together, and made us sit together in heavenly places in Christ Jesus." The renewing, the transforming of one's mind takes time. Be patient, but be diligent.

As the heart and mind are transformed, your life begins to take on the likeness of Jesus Christ in you. If we could work hard enough or act well enough, or in any way earn our way to heaven rather than it being a free gift from God through Jesus Christ, we would not need Christ to shed His blood, and die on the Cross as payment for our sins. The truth is no man can ever be good enough to enter the kingdom of heaven on his own merits. Either our service to God comes as an overflow of our love for Him, or it comes from a person who is trying to earn God's favor. We present our bodies a living sacrifice to Him, holy, acceptable unto God, which is our reasonable service. (Romans 12:1)

Haven't you heard people say; "I am praying, but God is not saying anything to me?" People pray all the time, even people who do not know Christ. Yet scripture teaches us lest you understand that the Holy Spirit dwells inside of you, you will not be able to understand how to listen to God and hear His voice loving you. When you hear the voice of a loved one, doesn't it light up your day, your life? You don't want to miss hearing the voice of your Heavenly Father. It does not get any better than that.

Many of you are just like me in Chapter Four, Christians who are not free in your own soul. The bad habits of the person you were before you knew Christ must be broken. There is restlessness, an unresolved, unsettled annoyance that follows you throughout your journey, like a cloud over your head. Our old thoughts and habits do not have the same nature as God and, therefore, cannot be joined with Him. He will not take your old thoughts and make them better. He will not "clean them up." He desires that you die to them, because you see the destructive way of them. Give up your stubbornness; you don't need those excuses for your unresolved emotions. When you are backed in a corner, make the hard choice to act and think as God does. Stop telling yourself, "I'm just going to do it anyway!" (Meaning you know there will be consequences, but you will deal with that later.)

"Grow Up!" Put on your Big Girl/Big Boy pants and man-up. All God, or anyone else for that matter, asks of you is for you to take responsibility for and own your sin. Then and only then can God set you free. We are like the little boy who brought his broken toy to his father and asked him to fix it, only the little boy would not let his father hold it.

Unless you know me, my life experiences are not going to make any difference to you. You have had hardships yourself! What I do hope will make a difference in your life is the principle of "How" God has used those experiences to speak to my heart about the information, memories, feelings, etc. I have programmed in my brain that are keeping me from being free. God sees every memory in your brain. He longs to help you see your way to the lies that are so painfully separating you from all you love and desire to relate to. God hears your heart's cry. His provision for you is already in place. Like any inheritance, we must do what is necessary to make it our own, only then can we enjoy what has been freely given to us.

Chapter Thirteen

THE LOVE OF CHRIST IS AN ACTION ILLUSTRATED THROUGH THE LOVE OF FAMILY, FRIENDS AND STRANGERS

One day you are healthy and the next day you find out there is something growing inside your body that will kill you. This is a time when you are deeply grateful for the time you have invested getting to know Christ and the love of God.

After a random complete body scan, I got a call from my doctor. "They have found a spot in your right upper lung and I want you to go see Dr. John Moore." I asked, "Who is Dr. John Moore?" I heard my doctor say, "He is a fine cardiothoracic surgeon; in fact, one of the finest."

My first thought was, "Great! I could have gone all day without this phone call." My second thought was "Okay Lord, I trust You and know whatever You have for me is good." I called a few friends and asked for prayer. Then I got on my knees.

Next thing I know, Ed and I are standing beside Dr. Moore looking at my X-rays. Four weeks later, I find myself awaiting surgery. Was I nervous? All I can tell you is God's loving arms were so encompassing me, I could best be described as being under a covering. A Holy Spirit covering. Those three to four weeks before surgery, I had gone about my days peacefully organizing my life as though there were a possibility my life would never be the same. My days were filled with continual conversations with my Jesus, abiding in the love of God that brought a smile to my face.

It is so funny to recall that I had even gone through my jewelry and made four separate little pouches, one for each of our grandchildren. (The things we do….) The peace of Jesus was with me from start to finish. My prayer life was a joy. My time with Ed was fun and exciting. I saw friends and family and there seemed to be no negative in our relationships. We were living that life of faith and love that Christ intends for us to live each day, every day. The things that had taken precedence before were suddenly unimportant.

They rolled me into the operating room with intravenous in my arm. It was ceiling to floor green tiles. I remember asking the man who was rolling me in, "Do I have to look at this? I don't really want to see it." And Boom, I was out like a light! God bless that nice man.

Five and one half hours later, Ed said to me, "Dr. Moore came out and told me it was "Rare" that he ever was able to tell a family that their loved one does not have cancer." Ed continued, "Dr. Moore says you do not have cancer! You had a rare, fast growing, bacteria in your lung, he removed it and you should be fine. No chemo, no treatments, just lots of rest." Ed was smiling all over his face. I was drugged, of course, but smiled and went peacefully back to sleep.

Our faithful friends who were waiting with Ed and our daughter, Adelle, joined Ed as he shed a tear of relief and gratitude.

Dr. John Moore is my hero. I hope God returns to him more than 100 fold all he did to give my life back to me. Jesus must not be finished with me yet, was all I could think.

During my nine days in the hospital, there were a few opportunities for human error and for God's angels to protect me. Someone forgot to remember to give me my heart med for three days, which made me feel like I was having a heart attack. (The nurse started asking for help in a loud voice.) Secondly, the culture they took from my lung and sent to the lab started looking like Tuberculosis. I was awakened to four people hovering around me unplugging everything and rushing me out of my private room into another small private room. Ed told me they thought I was contagious and he now had to wear a mask in order to visit me. They had also put a big X of yellow tape across my door that said "Quarantined. Do Not Enter."

Dr. Moore had inserted a drainage tube in my side that went down into my lung. The nurse who pulled the tube out forgot to put pressure on my body so as not to allow it to suck air in as she pulled outward on the tube. Consequently my right side blew up like a balloon and I could not breathe. Dr. Moore was called to my side. (This is when Ed and my sister lost it!) They refused to leave me and told Dr. Moore they thought I was NOT getting very good attention! Poor Dr. Moore. He not only had been on his feet operating all day saving lives, he had to deal with an irate family.

Jesus sent extra angels to guard over me and all obstacles were removed in a few days. The nurses were kind, but my sister and Ed would not leave my side, 24/7 the entire 9 days in the hospital. No one could have a better sister or husband to nurse you than I do. Devotion, sacrifice, hard work, loss of sleep, loving care and kind encouraging words exuded from them continually. My sister slept right next to me at night listening for me to breathe, as a new mother listens for her infant. I know she was praying over me. She even kept a journal of every person who came in my hospital room, their name, why they were in there and what they did while they were there. She kept the names of medicines given me and the dosages. She cleaned my bathroom with rags and Clorox from home, to prevent any staff infection. She brought me food, water, and Coke and helped me to the bathroom, over and over again. She helped me shower, brushed my hair and got the Chaplain to come talk to me after they overdosed me on antibiotics, giving me a horrible nightmare. (I dreamed demons were trying to kill me. My hallucinations were so real, I needed prayer.)

Seems I had caused everyone as much trouble as I possibly could have and now it was time to go home. The hydracodone kept me semi drunk for two months while I rested and gave my body time to heal from the inside out. Thank goodness Dr. Moore did not have to break my rib! During this time, my husband's love for me overflowed.

In my journal dated September 19, 2005, which was during my recovery period, I recorded; "Today is a very Special Day Lord; the day you have made. I rejoice in it. Thank you for Barbara being here with me. What a treasure her friendship is. She brought me a beautiful bouquet of flowers wrapped in lavender tissue paper, tied with a satin lavender ribbon. They were so feminine, they had

"Love" written all over them. Thank you for my friends Lord and thank you for all the loving care I received from my husband, Ed."

God sees it all. We trust in Him and smile at the future.

Christ's love illustrated to me over these two months came in many forms. A therapist was sent to our house to make sure I was getting some moderate exercise so I did not become weak. She was very cheerful and I noticed she had a great deal of patience. I thanked her for her sweet spirit because I was so, so slow doing what she asked of me. I'll never forget what she said; "Happiness is a journey, not a destination. The joy is in the journey." Complete strangers were used of God to speak to my heart.

I have a friend, a very close friend who God put in my life very early on. Her name is Helen Maddox. Helen and I have been friends for sixty-five years. Helen is the person who has taught me so much about the value of just "being." Just being present and still and together and quiet; just respecting the moment and the silence of our own thoughts, together. Through the years, we each have taken separate journeys, not always down the same path. Helen is very curious about so many things. She is interested in learning all she can about health and wholeness, ministry, God and people, and she is not afraid to take a hard look at herself.

Helen is a wonderful businesswoman with an instinct about investments. She speaks truth to me even if it is not my favorite thing. She is fun and is an encourager; she is selective and beautiful, inside and out. None to my surprise, Helen watched over me during my surgery as well as during the two-month recovery, visiting me at home showering me with prayers, gifts and love. Helen loves me, because she knows the love of Christ.

You have to listen to Helen when she talks to you because you never know when she will pop out with words of wisdom. She says things to me when I am pondering over something, like; "You were born with wings, why should you crawl through life?" Or if I am trying to decide on something, she might say, "Why don't you go ahead and take that leap? You may find out you can fly!" She never ceases to amaze me. How did I get so blessed to have a friend like this? Thank you Lord.

My two oldest friendships are with Helen and Jackie. We have been pals forever; traveling together, learning from one another, raising our children together, laughing together, and keeping so many years of deep confidences we can't even remember them all. The trust factor among us is incredible. God has truly given me His gifts in these women. They are His earthly extended hands of God's love and grace for which I am eternally grateful.
By the way, my body is all healed up! My lungs remain healthy.

God is good, all the time!

When I find myself walking on the beach or whizzing down the sidewalk on my joy rider tricycle, I look up at the heavens and say, "Thank you Lord Jesus for restoring my body and my soul. Now it is my turn to help someone else Lord, show me the way."

L to R: Helen Maddox, Roxanna Jordan, (a sweet friend we met along the way), Jackie Beavers, and Joanne Forrest Nutting

Chapter Fourteen

MORE PONDERING GOD'S ANGELS

My new friend Carolyn once asked me about angels. She complimented me and was trying to thank me for staying by her side while she was in the hospital. She called me her angel. My heart knew she appreciated my watchful, protective presence. I told my friend we would talk about angels one day if she would like to. She said she would like that very much. She had some questions she would like answered.

Carolyn's words blessed me in her sincerity and gratitude. I didn't really know how much she knew about angels, so I decided to seek God's word on this subject. As I pondered, I prayed for God's wisdom and His words to help my friend understand more about angels. I believe in angels as they have so watched over me all my life. God's word speaks of his army of angels, which is a whole book for another day. However, I wanted to be able to tell Carolyn about God's ministering angels, so I began to read.

God's Word teaches us in Genesis 1:27, that God created man in his own image. "So God created man in his own image, in the image of God created he him; male and female created he them."

Angels are spiritual beings sent by God to minister to people. From Genesis to Revelation, angels are referred to. Each of us is assigned angels to keep charge over us. Psalm 91:11, Isaiah 63:9 and Daniel 3:28 illustrate to us their protective power over man. Angels protected Shadrach, Meshach and Abednego from the fiery furnace. The angel brought them forth unharmed.

When Daniel was cast into the lion's den, scripture tells us God sent His angel, and shut the lions' mouths, that they have not hurt Daniel.

Further, Acts 12:7 teaches, "And, behold, the angel of the Lord came upon him, and a light shined in the prison: and he smote Peter on the side, and raised him up, saying, Arise up quickly. And his chains fell off from his hands."

Angels speak to us, protect us, and are powerful and plentiful. They appear to man when God commands them to. There are cherubim, seraphim, archangels and gathering angels, as illustrated in Matthew 13. When Jesus is speaking to His disciples and the multitudes, of the seven parables by the seaside, we see His reference to angels.

Christ uses illustrations for the purpose of clarity and understanding. In fact He tells seven different stories by illustrating with parables.

When we are trying to explain something that is a little difficult, to a child or anyone, we use illustrations to get our point across; illustrations made simple, illustrations on a simple level of understanding. The illustration might be called a parable. This is why Jesus illustrates with parables, so that the multitudes would be able to grasp the truths he was speaking of.

Please enjoy reading parts of Matthew 13 with me:
"The same day went Jesus out of the house, and sat by the sea side. And great multitudes were gathered together unto him, so that he went into a ship, and sat; and the whole multitude stood on the shore. And he spoke many things unto them in parables, saying, Behold, a sower went forth to sow; And when he sowed, some seeds fell by the way side, and the fowls came and devoured them up: Some fell upon stony places, where they had not much earth: and forthwith they sprung up, because they had no deepness of earth: And when the sun was up, they were scorched; and because they had no root, they withered away. And some fell among thorns; and the thorns sprung up, and choked them: But other fell into good ground, and brought forth fruit, some a hundredfold, some sixtyfold, some thirtyfold. Who hath ears to hear, let him hear. And the disciples came, and said unto him, Why speakest thou unto them in parables?

He answered and said unto them, Because it is given unto you to know the mysteries of the kingdom of heaven, but to them it is not given." (Meaning they had no way of being able to understand the mysteries of the kingdom of heaven because they had not yet become believers in Christ, the Son of God.)

(Skipping down to verse 36) "Jesus sent the multitude away, and went into the house: and his disciples came unto him, saying, Declare unto us the parable of the tares of the field. Jesus answered and said unto them, He that soweth the good seed is the Son of man; The field is the world; the good seed are the children of the kingdom; but the tares are the children of the wicked one; The enemy that sowed them is the devil; the harvest is the end of the world; and the reapers are the angels. As therefore the tares are gathered and burned in the fire; so shall it be in the end of this world. The Son of man shall send forth his angels, and they shall gather out of his kingdom all things that offend, and them which do iniquity; And shall cast them into a furnace of fire: there shall be wailing and gnashing of teeth. Then shall the righteous shine forth as the sun in the kingdom of their Father. Who hath ears to hear, let him hear."

Verse 49. "So shall it be at the end of the world: the angels shall come forth, and sever the wicked from among the just, And shall cast them into the furnace of fire: there shall be wailing and gnashing of teeth. Jesus said unto them, Have you understood all these things? They say unto him, Yes, Lord."

God's word speaks of angels coming forth with power from on high to cast multitudes into a furnace of fire. As you live your journey, may your heart, mind and spirit be quickened to watch for your personal moments when you know because you know, God's angels have taken charge over you in the way you most needed them at that moment.

There have been many times when I have been aware there were angels around me and around our children. The experiences of your own life, the experiences of your children's lives, and the experiences of your grandchildren's lives affirm to you that someone is protecting you all. Near death experiences that could have had a tragic ending, have turned out unexplainably well. Let me share with you one life experience I had not too many years ago.

One busy Sunday afternoon, as I was driving up highway I-95 on my way from Cocoa Beach, Florida, to Atlanta, Georgia, it was pouring down rain. This was just after hurricane Katrina had come through the United States. It was very dark with low visibility so I was slowing down from about 72 miles an hour to 60 miles an hour. The traffic all around me was flying by on this five-lane highway. About the time I noticed my speedometer reading 60 miles an hour, a red pick up truck flew past me on my right side. The young man driving must have been going 80 miles an hour. He hydroplaned, slammed into the right side of my car and knocked me into the next left lane of traffic. It is a miracle there was not a car beside me in that lane. In shock I eased my way over the three lanes of traffic on my right and came to a stop on a grassy shoulder of the highway.

I sat dazed and trembling and as I was about to call 911 I realized there was a police lady standing under an umbrella, next to my window. I don't know who called 911, which brought her to my aid. Evidently another motorist who saw the accident. I rolled down the window as she asked me to, and heard her say, "Are you all right?" I asked her to please look in the back seat and see if my dogs were alive, as my neck had already begun to stiffen. She said, "Yes, your dogs look fine; why did you call 911?" I told her I wanted to report that I had been in an accident. She looked at me puzzled and said, "Your car looks fine." I asked her to go to the other side of my car and upon her return she said, "Oh my goodness, you've been in an accident, but where is the other car?" I told her I did not know.

Soon we learned by way of her radio, that a red truck had spun out of control and come to a stop two miles behind me. (It must have taken me two more miles to work my way across the three lanes of traffic and come to a stop.) After answering all of her questions and filling out paper work, I made a phone call to Ed. My car was drivable, so Ed advised me to go to the nearest motel, stay the night there, and rest. I was pretty shaken by the impact.

Once the shock had subsided, I remembered the prayer I had prayed before I started the trip that morning. I asked the Lord to put extra angels around my car to take me home safely. I knew because I knew, God had done exactly what I had asked of Him, protecting me from what could have been a tragedy. Though I could not see God's angels camped round about me, I knew they had, with God's power, kept my car from turning over or from being hit by other cars.

Every day, every moment, I believe God's angels surround God's children. And if we remember to ask God for extra angels, God sends them immediately to us for our care and protection.

Danger lurks everywhere. There is no way to avoid the evil of mankind's mistakes. God knew from the foundation of time that mankind in our frailty would need His literal, functional covering of protection given by His angels. It is sad and hard to point out that non-believers do not have this powerful protection.

Like the parable of the good seed in a man's field, while men sleep the enemy comes. (Verse 24 and 25, "Another parable put he forth unto them, saying, The kingdom of heaven is likened unto a man which sowed good seed in his field: but while men slept, his enemy came and sowed tares among the wheat, and went his way.") You may be wide-awake, eyes open, yet spiritually asleep. We must listen to God's warnings and heed them. We must seek his face every day; we must pick up our cross daily as Christ tells us to do. We must put on the armor of God. (Ephesians 6:10-20)

Prayer is our continual vigil with Christ. Our continued dialogue of praising, seeking, asking, listening and obeying; spending time with Christ in his Word and in prayer is how we develop our friendship with him. If angels were not real, God would have told us so.

Fast-forwarding for a moment, I would like to share one other experience in my life when I was clearly aware there were angels present all around me. Over the years, as I grew in my understanding of Christ and of my self, Mama and I developed a wonderfully fulfilling and fun relationship. We truly were restored in God's love and enjoyed each other's company very much. We spent lots of time together having long, intimate, meaningful talks about Jesus and life. In addition, many a day, we shopped until we dropped! (Girl fun.)

So the night my Mother died in March of 2008, the unexplainable peace that passes all understanding abounded in my being. It abounded in my sister's life as well. We knew there were angels all around us; we felt their presence. We knew they were protecting Mama and had come to escort her home. It was the middle of the night. Mama was sleeping peacefully so I laid down to rest. Without my knowing, Mama woke up, tried to get out of bed to go to the bathroom and fell forward, hit her chase lounge and slid to the floor. No harm done except she slipped back into her semi coma, lying on the floor. Her little Maltese dog came in my room, stood staring at me crying and nervously paced back and forth until she literally told me to "get out of bed!" I got up and asked her what was wrong? She went running into Mama's room with me right behind her. There I found Mama on the floor, unharmed but asleep. God's angels had protected her in her fall. I am sure of it.

I called her name and woke her up. She was disoriented and asked me where she was. We got her back into bed and all was fine, yet Mama died within the hour. When she died, my sister knew immediately she had taken her last breath. The Spirit of God had left Mama's spirit. From under the bed, Mama's little dog let out a painful, verbal, knowing cry. The phone rang. It was Mama's nurse calling to ask if Mama was all right that she knew something was going on. The peace of Jesus was upon us in the middle of a powerful experience of death in the most peaceful form. We knew Mama's angels had come to escort her into the presence of God. My sister and I were not weeping and torn to pieces like I had always thought we would be. Instead, there was a Godly presence of caring and nurturing, and overwhelming love.

Nancy Susan and I covered Mama's sweet, still body with the bed covers. We hugged each other, and with a Holy Spirit numbness, quietly began to straighten things around Mama's house. We just wanted to be with God, with Mama, by ourselves. The tears have come many times since that night, all with a smile of gratitude. No regrets. Mama's last words to me a few hours before she died, were; "I love you, too." I believe when there are no regrets; the heart is at peace; even in the midst of a storm.

Keeping your eyes upon Jesus when all around you there is difficulty is an exercise in faith, yet nothing you are consciously trying to do. You just know because you know that God is with you.

There are times when God's power obviously has placed a covering over you where Satan cannot find his way in. God's angels are protecting you from any and all evil. This is when you are deeply aware of how limited Satan is. When God decides to restrain Satan, he becomes powerless. Try to remember, Satan cannot touch you, lest you let him, because you have the power of Holy God indwelling you, and many mighty angels that surround you to protect you.

May your angels bring you all the goodness of Christ every day and may you become more aware of them as you continue on your journey. To my very special friend, Carolyn, I dedicate this Chapter to you. I hope this answers a few of your questions and encourages you to begin your own ponderings. Then you can come and teach me the things of which I know not! That is what I call fun.

Chapter Fifteen

DO THE ONES YOU LOVE HURT YOU THE MOST?

Jeremiah 5:3, "O Lord, are not thine eyes upon the truth? Thou hast stricken them, but they have not grieved; thou hast consumed them, but they have refused to receive correction…."

Yes, oddly enough, it seems the ones you love hurt you the most. In nearing the close of this book, I share one last hard subject with you for the purpose of encouraging you in God's love and faithfulness. No matter how hard the path is that your journey is taking you on, try to remember, God is there with you.

Life is uncertain, regardless of who the President of the United States is, whether the Stock Market is up or down, whether this is a good year or bad, regardless of why, life is uncertain.

Whatever you are placing your trust in, your hope in, your identity in, if it is not Christ, when the winds change, you will find yourself on shaky ground. Today you feel secure, tomorrow your security is gone; today you are healthy, tomorrow you find out you are not. Today you are young, tomorrow, one day older! Nothing stays the same except Jesus.

Ed and I have been married forty-eight years. Am I secure in this? Should I be? Who knows what tomorrow will bring. People change as they grow older. There are deal breakers in every marriage and abuse is certainly one of those. There are different kinds of abuse: physical, mental, emotional, financial and spiritual.

Early in this book I mentioned to you that before I married Ed, I told him about my father and his physical abuse. And because of my father's abuse, I explained to Ed that if he ever hit me, I would leave him. No matter how much I loved him, I would leave him. He is too big and too strong and I could not tolerate any further abuse. I had to know I was safe with him and that he would not hurt me; he would respect and protect me. Abuse was the deal breaker for our marriage.

As I write, it is spring, 2009 and the economy is horrible in the United States. Bernie Madoff has ruined wealthy people's lives

146

according to the news reports. He has taken their money under the pretense of investing it for them and stolen or lost it. He has lied about their portfolios, the returns they were making on their money and has left them in ruins with nothing. I mean nothing, billions of dollars, just gone.

The stock market is at the lowest in 25 years. Real Estate values are at an all time low. People are losing their jobs daily. There are no new jobs; no one is hiring. Big corporations are dismissing thousands of employees in their cutbacks. Literally, thousands of people are losing their homes to foreclosure. Banks are closing their doors. The FDIC is being questioned as to its stability and ability to cope with all the losses.

Social Security is at risk of failure before our children reach retirement age. America is in the middle of fighting two wars. People in America are going through horrific adjustments.

God is shaking everything that can be shaken in order to establish His people in Him. It is as though God is saying, "Wake up!" "Are you serious about following me, or not?"

I ask you, have you become so accustomed to dysfunction and chaos that it has become your "norm?" Are you now insensitive to God because you are "used to" what you know, even though your life is killing you inside and out? As bad as your life is, could it be you don't make choices for change because you feel you are stuck. Are your eyes and mind blinded by excuses like, "I don't have anywhere else to go." Or, "I don't have enough money," or, "I'm too old to change," or even worse, "I know in time, he/she will change, if I just keep loving him/her."

Do you "settle for" the abusive way of life of your choice, and continue to do the same thing over and again that you have been doing for years? "Stinking Thinking" some people call it. Thinking that defeats your every heart's desire. Is there a father, a spouse, a friend in your life that continually controls you, either through manipulation or demand?

In plain English, are you being abused? When a life, a heart, has given first place to any other than Christ, whether it be to money, a controlling spouse, a ranting boss on a job you hate, a boyfriend or girlfriend who is using you….whatever, there is probably some measure of abuse in the relationship. If you take a look at the lies you are telling yourself in order to keep yourself sane while in your misery, you might be asking yourself "Why...Why am I living like this? Has God deserted me?" You might feel somewhat like you are going crazy.

The devastating cost of non-physical abuse to girls and women primarily is not pleasing to God. Not for one minute. We must realize the abuse will not stop until we agree with God, number one, that it exists, and two, that you have had enough, and this is not pleasing to Him.

It is not God that has failed to make change in our circumstance; it is our choice to participate in the evil of abuse that is causing us harm. I thought for years that God would change the people in my life who were hurting me. I placed my hope in their desire, their love of God, and decision to change. The day came when God showed me that I had "misplaced" my hope. I had my hope in another person rather than in Him. The day God showed me the "people" in my life may never change, no matter how much I love them or try to earn their love for me, he showed me I could never "do" enough to bring change in another person. They must desire to yield to God and begin the process of change within themselves. Only then will change come. As we have already discussed, God is ready, willing and able to show you truth that will set you free, but each one must choose to ask God to show them the truth that will set them free. Each one's heart must sincerely desire to see their sinful ways and decide to stop the abusive behavior. No one can change another. God wanted me to once again view my life through His eyes. My hope began to be restored as I gradually gave the ones I loved to

Him. My heart felt relief. God showed me I was never meant to carry this heavy burden.

The disrespect men have for women is a learned behavior, I believe. A sin handed down from generation to generation. It certainly isn't learned behavior from Christ. Babies are not born with mean behavior. Like any other addiction, abuse knows no boundaries. You can be from the nicest of families and have the best kept secrets.

Pastors across the country are preaching on the subject of rebellion, idolatry, and abuse. They are trying to help women particularly, find their way out of abusive relationships. It does not matter your color or creed, abuse is unacceptable. Abuse is not the life God has chosen for His children.

It takes a lot of courage to ask for help when you finally are able to put the label of "abused" on your life. It is embarrassing and shameful, not only to yourself, but to your family. The secrets of the abused, run deep and long and wide.

Are you a person who is living in the circumstance of never being allowed to have any money, or a little extra money of your own that you do not have to account for? Are you always made to ask or beg for money? Do you live under the stress of being and doing without while having bill collectors calling your home all day and night? Are you living without health insurance? Are your children getting sick or are you sick and cannot afford to go to a doctor for help? Are you unable to buy groceries to feed your children and your spouse will not allow you to work or ask anyone for help for fear it will make him look bad. (I am not talking about people who are struggling to make ends meet financially and are sincerely trying. I am referring to women who want to work to better their lives and are not being allowed to do so by a controlling husband.)

Does your spouse yell at you, call you names or tell you to "shut-up." Is he abusive to your children or withdrawn from them refusing to acknowledge their worth? Does he punish you by withdrawing from conversation with you, or storm out of the room and slam the door, blaming you for whatever is wrong? Is life "all about him?" Because in his mind he is never the cause of the problem at hand, is it automatically your fault? Does he demean you in front of your children, family or friends, making you the brunt of his jokes? Does he tell outsiders your human frailties and embarrass you publically? Does he flirt with other women in your presence, dance with them too long at a party, leaving you to sit alone for everyone to see, then acts like he did not do anything wrong and tells you, you are too sensitive?

Does your spouse tell you one thing and then do another? Then he tells you he did not say that? Does he promise to do something that is important to you and then changes his mind, or lies to you? Does he quote scripture to you in order to manipulate you into doing what he wants? Does he charm you with loving words and pull you into his arms only to push you away when he is done with you? Do you let him treat you this way because you love him and are still hoping he will change?

Just because you cannot "see" any bruises does not mean you are not abused. Your bruised emotions, your broken heart, watching your rejected children act out, you're silent suffering and pain, begin to break down your health. Many women stick it out, to find themselves dying of cancer or on prescription drugs for depression, or becoming alcoholics. Of course the abuser is still out there looking good, going about his wonderful self-life, with everyone around him feeling sorry for him because his spouse is "sick," never realizing what he is doing to her.

Admitting your life is one that is being lived under the control of another is upsetting to say the least. Seeing the truth causes our hearts to break, but you are relieved to be able to identify the abuse. To discover you are not going crazy in this paradoxical time is a good thing! The confusion begins to lift as you see the abuse for what it really is.

152

There are so many families that look great on the outside, but inside the home, behind closed doors, there is so much pain going on. Who would have ever thought my mother, sisters and I were being abused? After all, we lived a "privileged life." We looked good, put on a smile and kept on performing in ways that made our father "look great." We wore our "masks" very well. We were hiding behind life striped with pain.

I have chosen to address abuse because of the stressful time we live in. The news reports at night on television say there is a rise in abuse because of the unusual stress Americans are under. Children are suffering under the hands of stressed out parents; fathers who have lost their jobs and are finding themselves staying at home for the first time to care for the children while their wives continue their jobs.

I encourage you to take a hard look at your life. If it is not acceptable to God, it is not acceptable. Your life is too important to God for you to waste it. If you are not sure whether to call your life an abused life, you might get on the internet and look up the word "Abuse" or "Narcissism" or words that come to your mind. As you know, there is a "world" of information out there at your fingertips.

For those women who are living in a life-threatening situation, I can only encourage you to make a plan of escape and when you are ready, leave and tell someone. You will need to gather as much money as you can, your car keys, a credit card and cell phone if possible. Pack a small bag in preparation to never return, and be ready when the opportunity presents itself. You can call "911" in your City if you do not have any support. They will come and get you and your children and take you to safety. They will help you get the support you need.

God loves you and is faithful to lead you beside the still waters. You can make it in this world without being abused. Women are very resilient; most are survivors and more intelligent than we give ourselves credit for. You are worthy, because, "WORTHY IS THE LAMB" who dwells inside of you.

I pray today will be the beginning of a new life for you; a life high and lifted up as on a great tableland where it is easy to move about. God says you are His child. Who could be better qualified to be your caretaker than your Heavenly Father? It is your right to live in safety. I know you will succeed if only you will try. Though you cannot know what will come of your life the moment you decide to make a change, remember, God does, and He is faithful to show you, one step at a time.

154

God may not choose to remove your abuser. This is a very serious matter, but each of us can, in our own way, find deliverance if we cry out to Holy God for his protection as we decide we have had enough.

If your abuser really loves you, they will ask for help in changing their abusive ways. Yet, if they love themselves more, you are left to seek shelter and change for your own life. I encourage you not to wait one more hour. You are Special and the way you can know how Special you are, is because God did not create but "one" of you. There is no other one on the face of the whole earth, "Just like you." I pray you will get started today finding those wonderful plans God has for your life.

Chapter Sixteen

A GRANDMOTHER'S EYES SEE JESUS WITH SINGING AND REJOICING

Looking back, you might say my life has been full of "ups and downs." Yes, I've encountered a few bumps in the road of life, but that was yesterday, and yesterday is over! I have so much for which to be grateful. The life God has ordered for me in the beautiful mountains of north Georgia is much more than I deserve.

From the early days of disruptions, deaths, losses, illnesses, joys and sorrows, successes and failures, until now, God has and is continuing to teach me through the experiences of my journey. Yes, I still live in chaos from time to time. Life is not perfect. Yet when the storms come, my heart is better able to focus than ever before. My faith has been strengthened and my will to yield to Christ is almost automatic. Christ has taken my "grandmother eyes" and filled them with His truths for my life.

I can see Jesus in circumstances as well as in people's words. In Creation, I see God's beauty and majesty; and in upsets, I see His power and faithfulness. Things still touch my feelings, yet somehow in a different place, a place where Christ reigns, protects, guides and directs.

My joy has been made full in seeing God's presence in the lives of my children and grandchildren. The powerful, loving blessing of the voice of a grandchild saying, "I love you Grammy," is indescribable. God has seen fit to temper me over the years and mesh me into his creation, forming one out of two. In my years of seeking to know Christ, I am learning to understand how to recognize what stands in between my heart and God, and how to face it head on.

I laugh now when I lose things or forget things, rather than it causing discouragement. When I drop things and make a mess of things, I am able to laugh at myself. I tire a little more easily and am not as physically strong as I used to be. I take more pills, walk a little more slowly, and my needs are different. The pain life has allowed me; a few health issues here and there, have been used of God to give me a greater love and appreciation for Him and for others. I still get fussy sometimes. However, it does not last long. The best part is I have decided that Christ is who He says He is and He does what He says He will do. I am persuaded God's faithfulness is trustworthy, so what is there to be fussy about!

God has not only been faithful to help me with the issues in my life that kept me captive, but He is still working on issues I have not found the answers to. He continues to meet me at my every point of need.

People become more powerful in their elder years of vulnerability than they were in the arrogance of their youth. God has humbled me, protected me, and given me so much. God has done wonderful things in my life considering when I first met Him, all I had to give Him was my heart and my ability to cook. I encourage you to take whatever talent or talents God has given you, no matter how meager, and use them to serve Christ.

My heart has become more tolerant with time, yet it remains full of fire; the fire of God's love which never fails me. God has given me a measure of wisdom and lots of laughter and fun together with Him at my side, as He continues to direct and redirect my path so that I might be able to help others, bringing glory to His name.

Hebrews 13:9 says; "For it is a good thing that the heart be established with grace." God has given me a place of solace, a place so right for continuing my pondering the things of God. Yet, there is always more for a grandmother to see through the eyes of God. Christ continues to hold my hand and lead me on, and will until the day He takes me home. For this, and for you, I am forever grateful. My Heart has found its "Song," its message, the song of purpose and meaning in my becomings and doings. My song sings truth that God will instruct me and teach me in the way which I shalt go: God will guide me with His eye. I sing when I am able to pass along to another the faithfulness God has shown me in my life, guiding them into God's truth for their life.

Your heart too, can find its "Song," as you sit at the feet of Jesus, and ponder the things of God. May I encourage you to reach out your hand to Christ; to trust Him and believe He is who He says He is. To believe Him to do all that He says He will. If you have not invited Christ to forgive you of your sins and to come into your heart and become your Lord and Savior, I encourage you to do so. A simple prayer, a simple conversation with God, is all it takes. If God is not real, if Christ is not the Son of God, how will it hurt you? Yet if God is who He says He is and Christ is the Messiah, and you fail to recognize the Word of God as truth, your life will be forever separated from the one who loves you the most; the one who came and gave His life, so that you might have eternal life. God is so

160

good. His love is so real. I just know you will find Him if you seek Him with all of your heart! His eye is upon you, watching over you, calling you to His side as He did me. Try closing your eyes right now and talking to Him. God in His love is faithful to meet you right where you are, as He has met me, over and over again.

This is Grammy (Joanne Forrest Nutting) beside the seashore. Her heart is singing.

Uncle Lee Hamilton teaches Joanne how to fish. She caught a nice red fish but doesn't yet know how to hold it! So exciting.

PINNACLE OF DESIRE
STUDY GUIDE
FOR DECIPLESHIP

PREFACE

The first step in understanding the Word of God is to pray and give your heart to Christ as your Lord and Savior. If you have already done this, you are all set to continue. If you have not done this, the following information and suggestions for study will probably not make very much sense to you.

If you have not invited Christ into your life to be your Savior and Lord, and would like to pray a prayer of salvation and invite Christ into your heart as your Lord and Savior, the following is a suggested prayer for you.

"Lord Jesus, I acknowledge to you that I am separated from you through sin. I understand that God the Father allowed your death on the cross, Jesus, as payment for my sin. Lord, I ask you to come into my life, indwell my Spirit Lord, with your Holy Spirit, and forgive me of my sin. I invite you to become my Lord and Savior. I need to be born again and I believe You are the Son of God, who came to wash away the sins of the world. Please make your life real in my life today Lord. Thank you for hearing my prayer.

In Jesus Name I pray, Amen.

Because of the sincerity of your heart, and God's faithfulness, your name has been written in the Lamb's Book of Life. You do not ever need to question your salvation again. All you need to do now is get to know your Savior. There is nothing you can do to add to the payment God has provided for your sins in Christ's death on the Cross. There is nothing you can do to earn God's favor. Your relationship, your love, your friendship, is all God in Christ, desires from you.

164

Simply begin reading your Bible. A Psalm, a Proverb, and the Book of John are a good place to start. Go to Church this Sunday and get in a Sunday School class where you will meet other people who are hungry to know God, as you are. And by all means, tell someone you have just prayed and invited Christ into your life.

Pinnacle of Desire
Study Guide Instructions and Suggestions

Your journey to seek after the heart of God with all of your heart, whether you are just getting started, or whether you have been at this for a long time, wherever you are, just take that next step forward and begin.

The questions that are asked are all answered in the manuscript of "Pinnacle of Desire," however, the answers are for my life, not for yours. The purpose of this Study Guide then, is for you to bring the answers for your life to the page.

As an individual, or as a group, you can read the book one chapter at the time, or you can read the whole book and start the Study Guide at the end of your reading. If you are reading the book as a group, I recommend you read one Chapter at the time at home, and then use the Study Guide as homework to research your own heart accordingly. Then when you get together with your group, discuss the Chapter and your homework among yourselves. If you are reading the book individually, do whatever is comfortable for you. Don't forget to pray as you go, asking God to let you see your life through His eyes.

Get your book, a notebook and pen, and your Bible. After reading the first Chapter of "Pinnacle of Desire," turn in your notebook and answer the questions in Chapter One of the Study Guide. After writing down your answers, ponder these things of God and of your life. Meditate on them, and journal about your thoughts as the week goes on. Talk about your thoughts with someone in your group, or in your life, that you feel comfortable with. Ask questions of your leader if you are not sure about something or don't understand the scripture references. Read on ahead if you so desire, but do the homework chapter, by chapter in order to gain the most from your journey.

Turn the page and let's get started.

Chapter One

COME UNTO ME AS LITTLE CHILDREN

Question One: Do you recall when you began your walk with Christ? When did you give your heart to Jesus?

Two: What influences did your environment have on you as a child?

(Was there stress in your home? Divorce? Did you have a dog, other pet you loved? Were there other people around you regularly that you cared about? Did your parents play music in your home? What was your favorite activity to play outside?) Recall what it was like to live in your shoes when you were young. Make some notes.

Three: What influence does the environment of your youth still have on you today? (Do you find yourself repeating traditions? Is there something you can't tolerate in your life due to sad or uncomfortable memories of your past? What are they? Write them down as you recall them.)

Four: Did you grow up attending Church and or Sunday School? Did this influence you in some way?

Five: Did you form any judgments against anyone in your family while growing up? Who cheered you on with encouragement when you were little?

Six: How did God illustrate His faithfulness to you during this time? Has your faith been strengthened as you reflected and looked at your youth?
Write down your thoughts. Discuss these things in your group.

Chapter Two

LIFE IS WHAT HAPPENS
WHEN YOU ARE DOING SOMETHING
ELSE

Question One: How has your faith been tested? Has there been a serious loss in your life? How did this make you feel?

Two: Did you take the Lord with you when you left home to go out on your own? When was this? How old were you? In retrospect, has your courage to try new things been enlarged? In what ways has your courage been enlarged?

Three: What new responsibilities have you taken on? Are you learning new things about yourself? What are they? Keep your journaling going.

Four: Have you experienced sadness in your heart? Why do you think God allows sadness? (For example, the loss of a boyfriend or girlfriend, job, etc.)

Chapter Three

AND WHILE YOU ARE DOING SOMETHING ELSE, LIFE HAPPENS

Question One: What was your first "real" job? As you are gaining experience in the world, how are you growing in your relationship with Christ?

Two: Have you established a pattern of praying? Have you made your plans for a specific place and time for prayer? If not, do so, and don't forget to put a Bible, pen and paper, and devotional nearby. Be prepared to write down what God the Holy Spirit tells you. (Read your Bible back to God, talk to Him about what is on your mind, petition God for your family, praise Him for His goodness and presence in your life and find scripture to learn more about what is on your mind as the Holy Spirit brings things to your remembrance. Look up the scripture and keep notes on what it means in your life.

Three: Are you beginning to understand how your life is orchestrated with opportunities to "see" yourself more clearly? Ponder this and discuss it with the group. Where has your life taken you? Where do you want it to take you?

Four: Ask for help if need be, in order to search out God's word. If there are concordances or other study books that will help you, make your list and go to the bookstore. Go to your Pastor and ask him what books he uses. Write it down, or ask your leader to do this and come back and tell the class.

Five: God will put people in your path who speak words of wisdom to you. What are some of those wise "words" you have tucked in the back of your mind?

Six: Who are the people in your life that you most admire, those who have made a mark on your heart? In what way have they influenced you? What character qualities do they live by that you would like to build into your own life? Make some notes and ponder them.

Seven: What are your hopes and dreams? Journal about them and begin to pray over them.

Eight: Seek out someone to disciple you if you are not able to find your way alone. The importance of discipleship and accountability are paramount. There is always more to learn. Make a list of a few names that come to mind to help you. Pray over them, God will show you "who." Ask God to prepare their heart to help you.

Chapter Four

IRON SHARPENS IRON

Question One: Join a prayer group when you feel ready or lead a prayer group if you have had experience praying with others. List a few choices. Research what is offered in your area and your church groups. Talk about this in your group. This will help you learn to pray aloud and for others.

Two: Guard your choices when you are frustrated. Are there sins in your family that have repeated themselves from former generations? What are they? You are not alone in your disappointments, failures or pain. Reflect and journal about this.

Three: Do you ever say or think, "I am just like my mother, or father, grandfather, aunt, etc.? Who in your family do you resemble in your thoughts and actions, and how so? Is this a good thing?

Four: Are there courses or classes you would enjoy taking that would further your understanding of Christ? Research these and make a plan to attend. Make a list and discuss these with your family and your class.

Five: Make a plan to invest your life in someone else's life. If you have never led anyone to Christ before, you can use the simple prayer at the beginning of this Study Guide. Learn the scripture references you will need. A few from the book of John will do. Begin to pray for your unsaved relatives and friends. Make your list and as soon as possible invite them to hear the gospel presented wherever you think is appropriate. And by all means, begin the discipleship process with them.

The discipleship process is not always possible due to long distances between where you and the ones you lead to Christ live. This is why I was so motivated to write "Pinnacle of Desire" and the Study Guide to accompany it. More than once, I have had to leave a City after leading someone to Christ and could not be there to help them grow in their relationship with Jesus. Hopefully, Pinnacle of Desire will be helpful as a tool for you to give to others who desire to know Christ and grow in their relationship with Him.

Chapter Five

REDEEMING THE YEARS THE LOCUST HAVE EATEN

Question One: What messages are stuck in your "computer" brain from your parents that are not God's best for your life? What are some of the mistakes your parents made that you prefer not to repeat in the lives of your children? Write them down. (Remember, your parents were doing the best they knew how at the time. Forgiveness is a good thing!)

Two: Put action to your desires. When you illustrate behavior you know is not of God, take time to think when and where you learned it. What are your thoughts about this? After pondering, list corrections that need to be made. Discuss a few examples in your group. You are not alone.

Three: Talk to your spouse about the goals and principles you would like to build into your own life, as well as the lives of your children. If appropriate, talk to your parents to gain their wisdom. There are things we all wish we could do differently if we had the chance to do them over.

Four: Make a plan for the implementation of your goals and principles. Remember to keep a freshness in your life; what does not work can be adjusted and readjusted.

Chapter Six
ALONE WITH GOD

Question one: Do you dream about your dreams? Do you make plans to have more fun with your children? Simple times are great. Quality time with your family does not have to be expensive. A picnic in the backyard or a park, a bike ride together, whatever you dream up that you know they will enjoy. Start today. Discuss your choices with other parents in your group. You may be able to give and receive some fresh ideas.

Two: Does the love of family and friends when you are sick give you deeper insight into their love and devotion for you? Do something special for them today. You know what they like, and "how" to make them smile. If you are going to make them a bubble bath, be sure you have some bubbles!

Three: Why is it important for you to take time to read the Word of God, every day? Keep an open Bible handy on the kitchen counter, bathroom, and in your prayer closet (where ever you have designated in your home for prayer). You can make memory cards with one verse of scripture on each for your family. Hang one on the refrigerator each day. Ponder on the verse and talk about it with your family. You can make these cards with your children or your group.

Four: Why is it important for you to look for opportunities to serve Christ by serving your fellow man? There is always a need out there in a family you know. Keep your ears attuned and you will find great joy as you give. Bake a casserole if they are sick and take it to them. Rolls will do! When appropriate, pray with them during your visit. Pick a flower from your yard and add this love to your gift! Offer to pick a child up from school if their Mom is sick. When you make yourself available, God will show you where the need is. Perhaps your group can do this together.

Five: When illness is in your life, is it a time of sadness or a time alone with God? I pray you are well and healthy all of your life, as God intends us to be. Yet, if the day comes that you find yourself on bed-rest, remember God is there with you. Use this time to pray and talk to God. Ponder the things that are on your mind in your family. Keep your devotional handy, Bible too. Share in your group, or journal, if you are alone, how God has spoken to you during your time of bed-rest? Share your experiences in your group.

Chapter Seven

TEENAGE TO ADULT CHILDREN

Question One: Have your children ever mimicked you? Watch and listen; they will teach you and lead you in the ways God shall have you go. Be careful to make the necessary changes in your life before evil takes root in your child. Each one in the group can share a story of a time when your child mimicked you or your spouse, illustrating behavior that needed adjustment. (This will probably be fun and funny, yet convicting!)

Two: Do you know your children's friends? Try to get to know your children's friends early on. Guide them in their relationships. If you become aware an acquaintance is not a healthy one, redirect your child's path as soon as possible. Talk about the signs your children illustrate to you that let you know an acquaintance needs your attention.

Three: Do you know the parents of your children's close friends? Try to get to know the parents of your children's friends. You will gain great insight into the values their children hold. Make a plan to meet at a park, or be together for ice cream, after a school gathering. Observe, and remember, you too are being observed. Ask questions such as, "where do you go to Church?" Make a list of a few questions that would be helpful to give you insight into the family values when you are together with your children's friends and family. (This sounds very nosey, but in today's time, it has unfortunately become necessary.)

Four: What are some things you can do to build your children's self-esteem beginning at a very early age? (Compliment them; support them by being present at important times in their lives. Cheer them on every time they complete a difficult task. They don't have to be number one on the baseball team; they just have to play in the game!) Talk about ways you can do this among yourselves. Ask someone who has grown children how they encouraged their children when younger.

Five: How can you participate with your children in ways that will help them become better at what they are interested in? (Like Dad throwing the ball back and forth with their children. Play basketball together or Mom's teaching your girls how to fix their hair different ways, etc.) What are your children interested in? List what you can do to encourage them in getting better at it, talk about it and make a plan. Participate with them. If the children in your group are around the same age, maybe it would be fun to have a group exercise with the children.

Six: Do you talk to your children about what is on their mind? It is helpful to discuss subjects with other parents so you can realize you are not alone in this wonderful gift of childrearing. However, do not violate your child's confidence by telling something to others your child has shared in confidence with you. Find something for you and your child to be doing while you are talking to them, perhaps a game or cooking together, something to keep their eyes busy so they don't have to look at you in the face the whole time you are talking. Looking you in the
184

eye takes too much courage and they are already being courageous to talk to you.

Seven: Daily, one sentence at the time (not a lecture), build into your children who God says they are. What scriptures come to mind? Research this and bring them to your group to share.

Eight: Should you ask for help with your child if their life gets too hard for you alone? Don't be embarrassed to reach out for a helping hand. You are not alone, and your child's life is too important to you and to God. Make a list of people who can help and call them. If you don't know anyone to talk to, call your Church office. They can direct you to counsel that is free of charge. Men, offer to help with kids who do not have a Dad. Getting a group together to play basketball at Church or somewhere convenient may make a huge difference in a young man's life. What can your group do to help someone's child who is in need? Consider taking this on as a group project.

Nine: Do you know anyone's child who is "playing with fire" or fooling around with alcohol, drugs, sex, etc. at an early age? Pray for this child and ask God's guidance about speaking to their parents. You may save a life. Talk about the value of this in your group. Pray together for the one who will be reaching out to another, for God to prepare their way. This can be hard and challenging, but nothing is too hard for God. Help these parents come up with creative ideas to keep their children interested and challenged doing things they enjoy. Go prepared with suggestions to help redirect their path! Discuss.

Ten: Do you monitor the words you speak over your child? Try not to say anything to them that you would not want God to say to you. Ask for help in your group.

Eleven: Why is it important for you to pray for your children daily? Perhaps you could start a prayer group with other mothers (and Dads with other Dads,) who would like to come together to pray for their children and stepchildren. Stepmoms' and stepdads' should be careful not to pick up an offence against your spouse's children.

Your spouse's child will always be "their child" no matter what they do or say. Pray for and forgive them. It is the right thing to do.

Twelve: Can you forgive others, as Christ has forgiven you? This is Big. Make a list of those you have offended or who have offended you. Pray over your list, then go to them if there is any way possible, and ask their forgiveness for your bad attitude. (Do not write this in a letter. You need not document the painful past.) You ask, "WHY do I need to do this?" First and foremost, because Christ commands us to forgive as He has forgiven us and secondly, because we want to stand "right" with God through obedience to Him. Third, asking forgiveness of another, frees us to be blessed of God. It does not matter whether they accept our forgiveness or not. Our effort is made in obedience to Christ and He sees we have done all we can. (Don't repeat the offense!) We don't want to miss God's blessings on our lives. Share in your group your experiences of obedience. You will feel like a thousand pounds has been lifted off your shoulders in obedience. Try to remember, you are the only one you can change. The rest is up to God. Make your plans and ask for prayer support as you go.

Chapter Eight
THE EYE OF GOD

Question One: Have you begun to work through the process of forgiving yourself? Receive Christ's shed blood and death payment for you as enough!

Two: What need do you have for your excuses, for your ill behavior? Why do you need these excuses? How does this serve you? Ponder these things and talk about them. By now, you should be building a trust factor in your group. Journal about those areas in which you are stuck.

Three: What will it cost you when you agree with God to forgive yourself and others? Write it down.

Four: Are you arrogant without being aware of it? In what ways are you arrogant before God? Talk about this giving illustrations.

Five: What will you do about this idolatry? Stubbornness is not of Christ. (I Samuel 15:23)

Six: Have you made your list of the places you are stuck? It is only the unworthy in me that refuses to bow down to the worthy. Obedience is only possible between equals; it is the relationship between father and son/daughter, not between master and servant. Scripture teaches us in John 13, "Though He were a Son, yet learned He obedience by the things which He suffered." Christ's obedience was as Redeemer, because He was Son, not in order to be Son. Make your choices concerning your stubbornness of thinking you know better for your life than God knows (Idolatry).

Chapter Nine

SETTING AN EXAMPLE

Question One: When God opens a door, is it best we walk through it? Look for opportunities to serve Christ with whatever talents He has given you. What are your talents? Who could be helped by them? Talk about this among your friends and your group.

Two: Are you sensitive to the promptings of God's Holy Spirit? Are you listening as you walk through your day, expecting God? You may have a divine appointment set by God while you are in the middle of something else. Are you ready to give an answer for your belief in Christ? Take time to prepare yourself right now for a divine appointment. Get a few tracts from your Christian bookstore and keep one in you wallet or nearby. Become familiar with the tract so you won't get caught unprepared. Practice using the tract in your group. Pass it on!

Three: Have you begun to teach your children how to give of themselves to others? If they don't have confidence in a talent, teach them by practice. Everyone can do something!

Four: Do you tithe? Do you understand the importance of tithing? Do you know what God has to say about tithing? Look it up in God's Word with your group and discuss what God has to say on this subject. Yield to God's Word. He is faithful. Start today by teaching this to your children.

Chapter Ten
PLANTING A SEED

Question one: Who are your friends that seek after the heart of God? Consider meeting with them on a regular basis to share what God is teaching all of you. Arrange this important part of your life.

Two: Would it be possible for you to offer your home as a place to meet? If you are the hostess, have an extra Bible on hand in case someone forgets theirs. Have Christian music playing in your home when they arrive. Have notepaper and pens available; drawing supplies if you so desire. A cold or hot drink and a cookie would be hospitable as well!

Three: Are you writing down what God is showing you? Write down the principles He is teaching you. Write down homework He would have you do. Discuss.

Four: Can you see the value of starting a file folder or a notebook of the things God is showing your group? I only wish our group had thought to do this. Reflections of those nineteen years being present with God would be so powerful and meaningful today.

Five: How can you experience the value of praying in a group? Pray together. Just sit in a circle and allow each member to speak as little or as much as is comfortable. Pray for each other, your families, friends and yourself.

Six: Give your group a name. Select a scripture you love and your name will be in it somewhere! Keep your group small. There will not be time to have every one participate if the group gets too large. Yet, if others want to join, all in the core group must agree to have them join. Your group will become intimate at times and "trust" becomes an important factor. You can also split into two groups if the men would like to meet at the same time as the women.

Seven: How can you give others a helping hand in starting their own group? Invest your life in another's life. Discuss.

Chapter Eleven
GOD'S FAITHFULNESS

Question one: How can you develop your prayer life and take it to a deeper level? Ask people who have been at this longer than you have. Ask them how they have learned more about prayer. Perhaps invite one of them to speak or teach your group. Come together and discuss.

Two: What does Matthew 5:39 say to you? Illustrate, study and explore Matthew 5:39. Try to remember, every time you insist on your rights, you hurt the Son of God. You can prevent Jesus from being hurt if you take the blow. ("But I say unto you, That ye resist not evil: but whatsoever shall smite thee on thy right cheek, turn to him the other also.")

Three: What happens when you try to look for justice to be done in your life? This is a mind set. Practice thinking as Christ thinks.

Four: Have you ever wanted to take a mission trip? Why? If you have a desire to take a mission trip, you might look into receiving training in "culture shock," before you go. Your group can plan to get training together, as well as take a mission trip together. Discuss the value this would add to your lives.

Five: Is your cup half full, or is it half empty? Practice being grateful. God blessed you by simply allowing you to be born in America. Discuss what you have observed by just having been born in the particular area of the City you were born in. Expand your thoughts.

Six: When God calls you, no matter how hard it is, should you go and serve Him? What will be missing from your life if you don't?

Chapter Twelve

THE COMFORTER HAS COME

Question one: Do you know what "righteousness" means? (God's goodness made available to us.) Discuss.

Two: Do you know what "judgment" means? (Deliverance from judgment, because the prince of this world has already been judged) Discuss.

Three: What is God's purpose in the Trinity? What is the purpose of God's Holy Spirit? Discuss.

Four: Study and meditate on how and why God created you a three part being.

Five: Why, at birth, are we born separated from God? Teacher can answer, or class can discuss.

Six: Why then, do we have a need for a way to be provided for us, for restoration? And who then, is able to provide this way of restoration for us?

Seven: Is God's provision in the death and resurrection of Christ our license to freely sin? Why not?

Eight: Are we accountable for our sins, knowing we are forgiven?

Nine: Are there consequences to our sins that we alone must bear?

Ten: Do our sins hurt God? Do our sins hurt our families? How do our sins hurt us?

Eleven: Again, why do we forgive others? And who is our forgiveness for?

Twelve: How do we know God's Holy Spirit speaks to us? (John 16). Is our Spirit quickened to the voice of God? How so?

Thirteen Hebrews 7:25; Does God continue to live today? Discuss.

Fourteen: What new habit must we form in order to make better decisions for our lives? (How do we listen to God?)

Fifteen: Is it important to compare what is stored in your memory bank with what God's Word teaches? Practice this exercise. Discuss and journal.

Sixteen: Are your painful emotions separated from the memory that gave these damaged emotions to you? Try to think of one and connect the emotion to the memory. How does this make you feel when you think of the one who has caused you such pain? Ponder this, and practice putting memory and emotion together. Write down meaningful illuminations.

Seventeen: Is there any measure of unforgiveness attached to your memory? If so, you know what to do!

Eighteen: What is obstinacy? Is there any measure of obstinacy or perversity connected to your memory, or to your unwillingness to forgive?

If so, what is it that is keeping the need for your excuse to blame someone else?

Nineteen: Put a label on your area of bondage before it becomes a stronghold in your life. Go to the Word of God and see what He teaches concerning the area in which you are stuck. Discuss in your group.

Twenty: What will you do with the truth God has given you?

Twenty one: Do you know how God tells us we are to become like Him? "Be ye transformed by the renewing of your mind," that is, transformed into the image of Christ. Be patient, but be diligent. The renewing and transforming of your mind takes time.

Twenty two: What has God freely given to you that you have not made your own? Perhaps you should stop here

for a while and ponder. When you are ready, discuss this
with your group.

Chapter Thirteen

THE LOVE OF CHRIST IS AN ACTION

Question one: Why is it important to pray for your friends who are ill or facing surgery? Can you name three?

Two: Is prayer serving the Lord? Can it become your ministry? Discuss.

Three: How has God allowed your faith to be tested lately?

Four: Are you becoming that friend that you want in your own life?

Chapter Fourteen
GOD'S ANGELS

Question one: When you have a need to understand a truth about God, where do you turn to learn? List three resources.

Two: How do parables help you understand?

Three: What are some of the assignments angels have? List them.

Four: Practice asking God to send His angels to protect you and your family, every day.

Chapter Fifteen

DO THE ONES YOU LOVE HURT YOU THE MOST?

Question one: Who or what are you placing your hope in? Think about it and be honest with yourself.

(Write down the answers to the questions asked in this Chapter.)

Two: Can you see your life with new eyes?

Three: What corrections need to be made?

Four: How will you make them?

Five: Is your life acceptable to God? Are you strong enough now, to face a deeper relationship with Christ as you face others and yourself? Discuss.

Chapter Sixteen

SEEING JESUS THROUGH A GRANDMOTHER'S EYES

Question one: In what ways have the wisdom of your years changed your life?

Two: Have your experiences broadened your gifts and talents? What are they? How are you using them for Christ?

Three: Have you seen the value in becoming transformed into the likeness of Christ, is it becoming easier to yield to Him?

Four: Are God's truths more meaningful to you now? How so?

Five: Have you become more tolerant of others and yourself? If you see someone whose life is in a ditch, reach down and give them a hand up!

Six: Do you laugh at yourself more easily?

Seven: Have you discovered talents in yourself that you did not know you had? What are they?

Eight: Have you found your Heart's Song? (Your purpose: What you are supposed to be doing with your life?)

Nine: Who is the Pinnacle of your Desire? (Be honest.)

Ten: Life is a life-long journey. No one ever "arrives," or concludes their journey until death. Do you know, because you know, God is guiding you with His eye? Sing and rejoice, play some of your favorite music. Try going outside and flying a kite again. Look up and soak in the beauty of God's creation. Above all, be reminded of how deeply God loves you!

If He is not already, I pray soon, He will become the Pinnacle of your desire.

Intermedia
Publishing Group

Publishing That Works For You

Would you like Forrest Nutting to speak to your group or event? If so, contact Larry Davis at (623) 337-8710 or email ldavis@intermediapr.com.

If you want to purchase bulk copies of *Pinnacle of Desire* or buy another book for a friend, get it now at www.imprbooks.com.